My Summer With Elvis

Spiritual Teachings
From the King

by

Willow Harth

For Elvis

Table of Contents

1. He Touched Me *1*
2. There's Good Rockin' Tonight *6*
3. We're Goin' Up, We're Goin' Down *21*
4. Gospel Elvis *31*
5. Saturday Night and Sunday Morning *39*
6. Elvis Christ *51*
7. That Many-Splendored Thing *63*
8. Almost Heartbreak Hotel *78*
9. Love Him Tender *86*
10. The Love That's Wantin' t' Come into the World *98*

Epilogue *104*

Acknowledgements *125*
About the Author *126*

There is some kiss we want with our whole lives,

the touch of spirit on the body.

Rumi

1.
He Touched Me

My love affair with Elvis begins on a sultry Sunday early in June. About thirty of us are gathered at the Quaker Meeting House in Madison, Wisconsin. Sunlight dapples the plain wooden benches. As usual, there will be no song or sermon, just a deep listening in silence for the promptings of the still small voice within, what Quakers call "that of God in every man."

I am in Quaker Meeting because Allyn is. We don't live together, but he's my partner and closest friend. Wherever he is, I am likely to be there, too. He's here because he likes to check in with the silence and to keep regular appointment times. For thirty years he's been a Quaker and a Buddhist meditator. The silence he's meeting is not a bearded old man up in heaven. Allyn calls God "the Mystery." I like that, it's so spacious. In the silence, Allyn "goes home." There, he stops fretting about the past or anticipating the future and allows all this world's broken pieces to form a harmony. He finds infinity under one roof.

When I enter the silence, I'm more likely to encounter whatever my worry du jour is. Sometimes, if I pat the worry on the head and say, "I love you and I'll check in with you later, but I'm busy now," I'll get messages or a series of images, like little movies. Quakers call such messages *leadings*. I can't make those grace notes happen, but when the still small voice sings, I pay close attention.

Today I close my eyes and settle into the silence. I'm feeling restless and am having distinctly uncharitable thoughts: "Why are Quaker women so aggressively drab? You'd think God had created a world in shades of gray instead of Technicolor." I'm the only one wearing lipstick. It's bright red to go with my polka-dot sundress and red ballet flats. Then I start worrying about my son. He lives on Maui, but does business in Indonesia, right in the midst of terrorists, Tsunamis, and bird flu.

I look over at Allyn. He's breathing peacefully, already home. In profile he resembles Jimmy Stewart—tall and slim with a mane of silver hair. Finally, I let go and relax. After a while, images arise, unbidden. I find myself going down a long hallway presumably to meet the Mystery. At first I think that I should jettison my baggage—all my opinions and worries—but I sense that God does not ask this; I am to bring my whole self home. At the end of the hallway is a door. I open it. Sitting on the golden throne is Elvis.

"Utterly horrified!" is the only way to say my surprise. Elvis smiles. "God is in all things," he murmurs in his mellow Memphis drawl. "Right now, I'm showing up as your own soul's beloved."

Somewhere in my mind the memory machinery whirls. This has to be a mistake, an unfortunate cosmic joke. When bobby-soxers were screaming for Elvis, I was still in diapers. Later, I skipped right over Elvis and onto Bob Dylan and John Lennon.

Elvis asks, "Are you ready t' cleanse your heart in mine?"

"No." I shrink back, not at all ready to get with what sounds like a southern revival river baptism.

"Well, at least let me hug you, honey." Sensing my resistance, he adds, "Hugging's good for the soul. Touchin' hearts, we remember our oneness in God." His arms enfold me. The surprise of roses is everywhere. An ecstatic melting into joy. And then the sweetness of the love that loves one's neighbor as oneself. Elvis whispers, "This is the love that's wantin' t' come into the world."

I am shaking hands with the Quakers next to me. How has an hour passed? An Elvis sighting in Quaker meeting! I'm certainly not going to tell Allyn. It's beyond ridiculous. From an historical perspective, it's downright transgressive. Quakers aren't the direct descendents of the Puritans, but they are certainly kissing cousins. For early Quakers, sex was a necessary evil. Young men wore wooden contraptions to bed to prevent masturbation, and girls were admonished not to be temptresses. The ultimate Quaker virtue was, and is, simplicity. They have no rituals, no ecstatic music, no poetry, no painted idols. Quakers wouldn't have condemned Elvis the way most preachers did; they really do practice brotherly love. Elvis would simply have been beyond their ken. Why would any man wear diamond belt buckles the size of his head, gyrate like Salome, sing in Las Vegas, and gorge on food and drugs and sex and guns? No wonder he died of an overdose on the toilet. How could any of those things possibly bring someone closer to God?

I have no idea. What I do know is this: However sequined, satin-ed and vulgar he may be, Elvis has just orchestrated my very own experience of the mystery. In his radiant embrace, my restless discontent dissolves. I am graced, renewed, lifted to the stars and back.

Everywhere is here—raining joy and filled to the brim with love. It's ridiculous. It's improbable. But could Elvis have an inside track to "loving the lord your God with all your heart, and your neighbor as yourself?"

I once asked a local pastor if anyone in his congregation actually lived those words. He laughed ruefully. Later, over breakfast at our favorite hang-out, the Edgewater Hotel, I told Allyn about the pastor's response. "It would be funny, if it weren't for the consequences," he said, pointing to a *NY Times* article headlined, "Car bomb In Iraq Kills Sixty." He tapped his chest. "The world is as we are. You have to be right with your own heart or your neighbor may be in serious trouble."

My own heart is a bit of a crapshoot. I can cycle through loving-kindness, neediness and meanness several times a day. Maybe Elvis knows something about love I don't. Or maybe I'm about to sail off on the ship of fools and become the biggest fool of all. Still, when a big-sky vision drops by—real or imagined—I'm not slamming any doors. I have no idea where this dance is going, and Elvis wouldn't be my partner of choice, but when he reaches his hand out to mine, I reach back.

He was as big as this country, as big as its dreams.

Nothing will ever take the place of that guy.

It was as if he came along and whispered some dream

in everybody's ear and we all dreamed it.

Bruce Springsteen

2.
There's Good Rockin' Tonight

By the second week in June, my summer with Elvis has become a full-time job. I feel seized by a compulsion that rapidly turns into a full-blown obsession. The timing is perfect. Allyn is semi-retired, so he spends much of the summer at his cottage in Michigan's Upper Peninsula. He comes back every few weeks to keep up with his clients—writers and artists and masters of the universe who don't need the kind of tending many psychologists' clients do. I've just finished my manuscript, **The Educated Heart**, which incorporates the new neuroscience and psychology of emotional intelligence into a spiritual approach to parenting. There's nothing more I can do with it until some agent says "yes." I'm a therapist, so I have some control of my time. Elvis sucks it right up.

Once I let Elvis into my life, he seems, almost thirty years after his death, to be everywhere—from *New Yorker* cartoons to serious feminist essays. The Discovery Channel named him in 2005 one of "The Ten Greatest Americans," in the company of Lincoln, Washington, and Martin Luther King. Alive, Elvis was the top-selling recording artist of all time; according to *Forbes Magazine*, he's the number-one selling dead one. Leonard Bernstein said of him, "Elvis is the greatest cultural force in the twentieth century. He introduced the beat to everything. It's a whole social revolution—the 60's comes from it." How have I missed this cultural icon?

During the day, I read Elvis biographies and gaze at his photographs. I keep the books hidden in my desk drawer and sneak peeks between sessions with my clients. I usually dread driving home after work. With the summer road crews out in force, a ten-minute ride home can easily stretch to an agonizing forty. Now, I can't wait to get in the car, slip in a CD, turn the volume up all the way, and travel along in my Elvis bubble. His early rocker, "Baby Let's Play House," practically lifts me out of my seat. "Don't" envelops me like melting caramel. I notice my mouth waters every time I hear it.

In the evening, I dim the lights and mainline CDs. My hands actually shake as I press the play button. How can dancing with a dead man be so thrilling? He's right here just like he was in Quaker meeting, only now his voice kisses every inch of my skin; his rhythm pulses every cell. Each song invites me to dance. Two hours later, exhausted and exhilarated, Elvis and I and the beat rise to the roof like Chagall's floating lovers.

The good feelings get up in the morning with me. I sing and dance my way through the day. Everywhere I look, everyone I see, shines. I feel absolutely delicious, just like the poet Rumi: "Put on God's eyes. See God everywhere/ No tiredness, no jaded boredom!" On my morning walk the sun fills up the tulip communion cups. Bluebells tinged with pink sway like lingerie on a line. Spring has come late this year, but the flowers have finally arrived. The squirrels I previously dismissed as rats with tails scamper as effortlessly as high wire walkers among the treetops. In the grocery line I look in the cashier's eyes and smile. She smiles back. I am amazed at the abundance of life—all these people we don't know who make our lives run well. My clients, whose self-absorption sometimes drives me crazy, I now recognize as none other than the latest expression of the awesome and enchanting universe. I sense I could be going off the Elvis deep end, but it feels so good I don't care.

Making dinner with my roommate, Claudia, in our kitchen, I'm still singing. She laughs at me. "What are you so happy about? It's positively un-American."

"I'm beyond happy, I got the joy, joy down in my heart." (I'm a word junkie, so I know there's a big difference between happiness and joy. According to Webster's, *happiness* is about luck, *joy* is an "exaltation of spirit.")

"Okay, so what are you joyful about?"

"Elvis. I'm spending a lot of time with Elvis. I think I'm in love."

"Elvis? In love with Elvis! You've got to be kidding. He stole everything from Chuck Berry? He was probably a racist. And musically? He's not even up there with James Brown."

Although I went to college on a debate scholarship, I'm not ready to argue with Claudia. She's a professor at the U-W Madison and teaches a class in Afro-American music and dance. Besides, I have my own doubts about Elvis. Only the joy is keeping me true. Our nightly trysts continue. What will the neighbors think? I already know what Claudia thinks, which is why I'm listening to Elvis in the evenings, when Claudia is out on dates or rehearsing. One of the reasons it's easy for us to live together is that we keep different hours. I get up at dawn and am in bed by nine. Claudia is also a performer and choreographer, so she's up at noon and to bed long after midnight.

We live in her house on an idyllic, tree-lined street, straight out of a **Dick and Jane** early reader, surrounded by families with a mom, dad, and kids. Our neighbors, tolerant as they are, are already a little nonplussed by the steady stream of men to our house. Most are the drummers and dancers Claudia works with, but she also has a lot of dates. She's almost sixty, but still beautiful—with wild black curls, a tiny waist, and oak tree legs. All she needs are two snakes in her hands to pass for a Minoan goddess.

Her joy is irresistible. Allyn refers to her as "God's little party girl," which is a bit of a misnomer, since Claudia is almost six feet tall. Our shoes lined up by the front door look like Mutt and Jeff—mine are a six, hers a twelve. She calls me "princess" because I'm fine-boned. It's not really a compliment. Despite my hourglass figure, she thinks I'm way too skinny. My social life is nothing like hers. Allyn is the only man, besides my close friend, Harvey, who comes to visit me.

I'm grateful it's early June in Wisconsin. The days are hot, but the nights are cool enough for me to close the windows. Elvis and I can be alone. I'm in my favorite nightgown. Yards of white cotton flow from the tight bodice almost to the floor. Delicate pink ribbons trim the neckline and hem, and tiny white buttons, just waiting to be unbuttoned, demurely line the front. As I dance around my room, I catch a glimpse of myself in the mirror. It's a shock—blonde hair askew, my nightgown drenched in sweat—I look like Glenda the Good Witch undone by an orgy. I look like someone wildly in love. But I've been wildly in love with Allyn for fifteen years. I can't quite fathom the grip Elvis has on me.

****

I met Allyn after he came to one of my art shows. I'd airbrushed a series of pieces in turquoise and purple. I learned later that my picture of two women standing— one pregnant with a belly like the full moon waving a cloth and the other holding a cup—had caught his eye. It came from a dream I'd had of two women preventing a deadly hurricane by offering a gift to the waters.

Afterwards, Allyn called to say how much he liked my paintings and to invite me to his condo for tea. "Wow, a buyer," I thought. That night I had this dream:

> *I open the door into a magnificent open space. Everything is an almost blinding white—white carpets, white wall, white marble fireplace. The entire room faces a lake. Sunlight blazes. I move towards the fireplace as a flock of gulls flies by. My mother is standing beside the fireplace. She says, "This is your true home." But all is not completely well. In the kitchen there's a sulky, slightly hostile teenage boy, and the bathroom stinks because the toilet won't flush.*

The next day I headed over to Allyn's, portfolio in hand. He lived in a pricey condo overlooking Lake Monona. This was promising. I was anxious to sell. As I walked down the hallway, I saw a pearl hatpin on the carpet. I picked it up and stuck it in my sweater. It seemed like a good omen. The invitation to my show featured a drawing of a being I called "pearl woman." I thought the pin would be a great conversation starter. I knocked. The door opened. I instantly forgot my paintings or the pin, because I had walked right into my dream.

Everything was white and filled with light. I walked over to the marble fireplace and a flock of gulls flew by. I didn't know anything about Allyn, but I felt compelled to tell him my dream. "But of course," I laughed nervously, "this isn't about you, because there was also a dangerous teenage boy and the toilet didn't work."

He smiled. "Well, actually I'm just a teenager. I've only been on the path of the heart for fifteen years, and the folks who built these condos skimped on the plumbing—my toilet always has problems."

He indicated that I should come over and sit on his big comfy couch. He brought out a tray of chocolate-covered ginger and a steaming pot of my grandfather's favorite tea, Lapsang Souchong. (It is because of my grandfather and his travels to China that my name is Willow.) He pointed at the candies. "Geshe Sopa, one of the Dalai Lama's teachers, thinks these are the perfect food. The ginger tastes like heaven and the chocolate tastes like earth." He didn't mention that he knew both Geshe Sopa and the Dalai Lama, or that Geshe Sopa had invited him to become a monk.

"So tell me, do you often dream like that?"

"Yes, since I was a kid, I've had pretty amazing dreams. But they're always a little wacky—like I have an inner Oracle of Delphi who's hooked up with Lily Tomlin."

"That surprises me. I've been a psychotherapist for thirty years. The only people I work with who dream like that are Native-Americans."

I laughed and extended my hand. "Well, meet the blue-eyed Navajo." I told him that I had spent my childhood between Toadlena and Two Gray Hills on the New Mexico side of the Four Corners Navajo Reservation. My mother was escaping a bad marriage. She had left my father in New York and headed out to New Mexico to teach at Nava Day School, a one-room schoolhouse in Newcomb. At first, the Navajos were suspicious of her, especially of her white-blonde hair. They called her Bellegona—white witch—but she won them over. Unlike most Anglos, she was quiet and respectful of the old ways. I was not quite two years old and needed a caretaker. My mom chose Nellie, a young Navajo woman. Mom told me much later, "Navajos never yell at children or hit them. That would offend the Yeis (the Navajo's guardian spirits). I knew Nellie would be good to you."

Nellie had a son, David Yazzi, just my age. She was also the grandniece of Hosteen Klah, the Navajos' most revered medicine man. He had never married and had no nephews. Although Hosteen Klah feared he'd be struck by lightning for giving away men's secrets to women, he'd shown his nieces how to weave spirit rugs. For traditional Navajos, activities are strictly segregated by sex and this kind of weaving was man's work. Nellie wove spirit rugs, too. She came to trust my mother, so we were often invited to the Yei-bachis and Chantway healing ceremonies that ritualize the complex and sophisticated Navajo way of life.

I was much too young to understand what the ceremonies meant, but I absorbed something of them through Nellie. She held me in her lap outside her eight-sided hogan beneath a sky of stars. The pungent scent of sage punctuated the dry desert air. A sick man lay on the dirt in a painted circle, while the Medicine Man pounded his drum and sang in a high voice. Navajos call the earth Changing Woman. They run to the east every morning at dawn to greet her and the sun. With Nellie, I felt I was in Changing Woman's arms and that the sound of the drum was her heartbeat.

Traditional Navajo life is guided by Hozcho, which means "to walk in beauty." Every thought, every feeling, every action leads you on the path of beauty or takes you away from it. To walk in beauty is to have a loving and wise heart. Hozcho dictates what you eat and wear, how you work and play, and how you pray. All of these actions prepare you to receive the deeper guidance of the Yeis, who speak through dreams and through the earth itself. A Navajo listens respectfully to the wind, the yucca, rattlesnakes, coyotes, hawks, the mountains, and his or her own dreams. Receiving dreams and visions and acting upon them for the good of the people (Navajos call themselves Dine, which means *The People*) is the ultimate expression of Beautyway.

    I told Allyn that it wasn't as if Nellie taught me to dream. I learned by osmosis, the way young children always learn. Her traditions simply seeped through my skin. When I was six, we moved to Albuquerque. My mother taught at the Indian School and I started first grade. I didn't see much of Nellie after that, except for brief visits in the summer.

    I talked on and on, even though I knew this was no way to sell a painting or to get to know Allyn. But he listened. His listening felt like lovemaking. He listened to me as if he were inhaling a rose he wouldn't dream of picking—delighting in every petal and each drop of dew, marveling over every thorn. The bright light had faded. Everything in the dusk-touched room glowed from within. Finally he said, "Beginnings are so important. Good or bad, they set the pattern for a life. You are lucky to have fallen among Navajos." He took my hand to help me up; it was time to go. "Let's meet at the Edgewater Hotel tomorrow for breakfast," he suggested. "For the price of an egg and coffee you get the most spectacular view in Madison." At the door he asked if he could hug me. I pressed against him. He pulled back. The pin; I'd forgotten the pin. It had stuck him in the chest, just above his heart.

Allyn wasn't looking for a relationship. He'd been married and had grown children. All the people he admired now—The Dalai Lama, Thomas Merton, Krishnamurti—were single. There was no way my waking self could have seduced him. But the pin did, and the dream. He called events like that "synchronicities" and added, "If you know how to look, they're everywhere." What has kept us together is our mutual obsession with questions we can't seem to stop talking about: Who are we? How do we live and love well? Why do we suffer?

Allyn's search for answers took him into science, psychology and meditation. When he was in his thirties, the book *God Is My Adventure* inspired him to go to India. He checked out various ashrams and gurus and met with the Dalai Lama. He studied with Krishnamurti in Switzerland and then with a Christian disciple of Gerald Heard (an English mystic and Aldous Huxley's teacher) in the U.P. He seems to know, or know of, anyone who is seriously pursuing the same questions. His brain waves have been measured with those of other meditators by the defense firm, McDonnell-Douglas. It sounds pretty cerebral, but he described his search this way: "I'm just checking out the joint." I loved his humor and refusal to get stuck in rigid beliefs. That's what made me trust him. "I'm not interested in believing in God," he said, "I want to know God." That expresses itself in his life as an incredible kindness.

I'm a sucker for a good heart. That's why I married both my husbands. Later, I discovered their kindness came more from the outside-in than the inside-out. My first husband was a seeker who went through several gurus before and during our relationship. He was kind because it was the right thing to do. My second husband's kindness came from existential despair: "If this is all there is and it's so grim, the least we can do is to be nice to one another." But Allyn's was different. His felt utterly spontaneous, as if he actually experienced other people as being himself.

My mother's dream words were right. Allyn—who he is and what he knows—felt like my true home.

Later, I would find out there was one room in that house where Allyn didn't go. It was a place of play and delight. Allyn, like all the people he admires, is a bit of an ascetic. I wondered if this was an occupational hazard for male spiritual seekers. In tender moments, if I said, "I love you," he would say, "I care very much for you, but I don't believe in special relationships." He meant that from a spiritual perspective what we love in another person is their inner light, not their particular personalities. That light is the same in everyone.

I, on the contrary, believe that in that room of joy every particular is exalted, like finding the world in a grain of sand and the ocean in a drop. I wasn't sure how to enter that joy myself, but I felt no spirituality could be complete without it. In fact, I felt that the love and enjoyment of this body and this world—and of each unique person in it— was the gift that women offered to all the patriarchal religions from Christianity to Buddhism.

There were, however, so many other rooms to explore with Allyn, it would have been ungrateful to hold this against him. And I didn't.

****

A few weeks into my Elvis mania, Allyn calls from his cottage. This seems like the time to tell him about Quaker meeting, my obsession, the books, the photos, the all-night dancing. I still feel uneasy, and I want his approval.

"Well," he laughs, "you're always wandering off on the road less traveled and relationships are a great way to learn about yourself. But Elvis's a bit of a stretch isn't he?" I tell him I agree.

His tone softens. "Look, you've never gone wrong following your dreams. That was a pretty big Elvis vision, and a vision's just dreaming out loud. If you're looking for my permission, you've got it. Go ahead and dance with the guy, just save the last dance for me." He is joking, but I know what he means.

Mythical archetypes can become spiritual partners

with whom we engage in soul-making

and the redemption of ordinary time and space.

Jean Houston

3.

We're Goin' Up, We're Goin' Down

For now, Elvis and I remain an item. At night, he follows me into my dreams. Early on, I dream I am in a huge amphitheater watching women in skimpy scarves dancing wildly on a hill. A dark young man seems to be inspiring them. Suddenly, in their frenzy, they begin to tear him apart, as if the only way to become one with him is to eat him. Then, in that weird way dreams work, I'm watching myself cradle his bloody body in my arms. Somehow I know it's Elvis and we're in some parody of Dionysus and his groupies, the Bacchae.

What can Elvis and Dionysus have in common? A lot, I discover. I invite my friend Harvey over to tea, so I can ask him about Dionysus. We sit outside in Claudia's gazebo shaded by two tall spruce trees. A cardinal's nest with chicks is hidden inside the smaller one. I pour Harvey tea to the sound of their chirping and think how out of character he looks in his black jeans and black cowboy hat. Harvey is a Jungian analyst and a former Lutheran minister. Everything about him—his soft eyes, salt-and-pepper hair, even his slightly melancholy expression—telegraphs kindness. My friends refer to him as Mr. Dear.

As a Jungian, Harvey is interested in the ways that mythical Gods and Goddesses represent particular human aspects and possibilities, as if each of us has an inner aggressive Mars, a seductive Venus, an intellectual Athena. He tells me that Dionysus, who is both very feminine and very masculine, represents the energy of ecstasy—transcendent release through the body and the senses. When our inner Dionysus wakes up, we feel radiantly alive and joyfully connected with every living thing.

"Sounds like sex, drugs and rock 'n' roll," I say.

"Well, for the Greeks it was a religious thing. The Dionysian rites used ecstatic dancing and music to bring the spirit down into the body."

"Paradise now, not when you die."

Harvey nods. "Dionysus," he continues, "is all about emotion, intuition and ecstasy." He is the mysterious beautiful stranger who slips into town, full of fragrance and song, seducing the women with his sweet delights. The men are enraged, but the women go wild, leaving their husbands, children and all responsibility behind to follow him. They get so carried away, they end up killing anyone who tries to stop them.

I tell Harvey that Elvis's early shows have been described as the wildest series of performances ever seen in show business. He leered, rolled his eyes, and moved like a madman. Adults were beside themselves. Elvis was denounced from pulpits. Critics jeered. Ed Sullivan showed him singing only from the waist up. In St. Augustine, Florida, policemen ringed the stage to insure that Elvis didn't move his pelvis. He taunted them by only moving his right pinky. The girls fainted and screamed and tried to tear off his clothes anyway. They rushed the stage, pummeling the police. A terrified Elvis, scratched and bleeding, was found sitting on top of a bathroom stall with nothing on but his pants, surrounded by girls trying to tear them off. One swooned, gasping, "Elvis is the most beautiful piece of forbidden fruit I ever saw."

And he is beautiful. Looking at the early photographs is like seeing Michelangelo's David come to life with a hint of Elizabeth Taylor's black-lashed beauty and sensuous curves. Elvis glows. He's classic and romantic, masculine and feminine. His androgyny is startling. In high school he permed his hair and wore make-up, ruffled shirts, and hot pink pants he bought in the black section of Memphis. Remember, this was 1955, and Elvis wasn't gay. His 1955 Nashville debut with the Grand Ole Opry was met with hushed disgust: Who was this guy moving like a black man and wearing mascara? He was the rebel without a cause, all menace and cool, and also the sweet shy choirboy you wished would make a pass at you.

Dancing with Elvis later that night, I sense all of this and an intangible something else. Maybe it's the fragrance of paradise, I think, remembering the roses in my Quaker vision. I don't feel like a hot chick getting ready for some heavy breathing, I feel like a temple dancer. Something about Elvis brings my soul right into my body or else lets me know it's been there all along.

Maybe Elvis is the latest incarnation of Krishna, the Indian God who fills this world with heavenly delight by playing his magic flute for the lovely lady Gopis. They number in the thousands, but he plays to each one alone, dispensing spiritual and sexual ecstasy.

Krishna has jet-black hair and wears makeup. His clothes shimmer with jewels. Scarves and flowers adorn his body. Elvis, too, as he matured dyed his hair black, dressed in jeweled jumpsuits, and wore scarves that he draped around the neck of any fan lucky enough to get a kiss.

In a photo from his 1972 global telecast from Hawaii, a bejeweled and lei-bedecked Elvis stands in majesty, holding his microphone like Krishna's flute, surrounded by adoring hula dancers. I place the photo on our refrigerator next to a picture of Krishna playing his flute surrounded by Gopis. Claudia notes the eerie similarity, but her views on Elvis remain unchanged.

One evening when Claudia is out of the house, I watch a DVD of Elvis's 1968 Comeback Special. I'm struck by the way the music overtakes him. In the "If I Can Dream" finale, Elvis's eyes bug out and he shakes uncontrollably, as if possessed. When it ends, he looks out at the audience with a "what the hell just happened to me" expression. The look is not self-possessed or triumphant. It's oddly imploring and shy and also spent and exhausted, as if he has been the flow-through for a force that's burning him alive.

Elvis described it to his friends this way: "When I'm singing, it's like a surge of electricity going through me. It's like making love, but it's stronger than that. Sometimes I think my heart is gonna explode." His account sounds like Hindu descriptions of the kundalini experience that signals a meditator's union with the divine. The kundalini is an electric-like energy that rises up through the spine with the exploding force of an orgasm. Maybe my imagining Elvis as a new Krishna isn't as wacky as Claudia thinks.

****

My book group meets once a month in the summer. We call ourselves the "Search Party," with an equal emphasis on search and party. Tonight, Malynn is here, also Margaret, Hedda, Odessa, and Harvey. Malynn is our youngest member, the daughter we all wish we had. She's just finished getting her M.D. Margaret, our eldest, is an editor at the university. Hedda is an artist. Odessa is often not with us; her work requires lots of travel. "Work" is probably the wrong word. Odessa is passionate about food. She's just been awarded an honorary doctorate by the UW-Madison for her efforts to make our relationship to food—the way we grow it and eat it—sustainable. My friend Harvey is the only guy in our group. Jungians believe the soul is feminine. "The only reason you're here," we tease him, "is to get pointers from us."

We've just finished Carol Christ's *She Who Moves.* We read her book after finishing *The DaVinci Code,* which depicts Mary Magdalene as Jesus' wife and the mother of his child. Reviewers described it as a feminine-friendly reinterpretation of the New Testament. But the plot was so complicated and the writing so stilted, we decided to take our feminist theology straight. Carol Christ is a feminist theologian with a Ph.D. from Yale. In this book, she reconciles the Christian narrative with sensuous pleasure, delight in this world and love in all it guises.

Tonight, we start Jean Houston's, *The Hero and the Goddess*. It's my turn to read the introduction. I begin: "A cultural hero dredges up something forgotten by a whole generation or even a whole civilization. He is a boon bringer; he becomes an inspiration for an entire culture." I can barely keep reading, my thoughts are racing so fast. A cultural hero? Can I talk this way about Elvis to my friends? Isn't he the Godfather of the sixties and all the movements from feminism to ecology to New Age spirituality that came out of it? "The first time I heard Elvis it was like busting out of prison," exalted

Bob Dylan. For Little Richard, "Elvis was an integrator, a blessing…He opened the door for black music."

I'm starting to think Elvis did a whole lot more than sing black and white together, or pave the way for the sixties. He remarried body and soul. Elvis released feelings centuries repressed. He announced to a head-heavy, rule-bound, segregated, and puritanical 1950's white world that the freedom train was a-comin' with a rock 'n' roll beat in the driver's seat. One critic said, "Elvis brought us a dance it took a whole civilization to forget and ten seconds into his first Ed Sullivan show to remember." I love that line at first sight and immediately tape it on the fridge under my Elvis/Krishna montage. I feel so sure Elvis is calling us into a sexy spirit-filled body. I know he's calling me. I can't prove it yet; I don't even know if Elvis had a spiritual life. I only know how I feel.

After I finish reading the introduction, I wonder why I don't want to reveal my thoughts about Elvis to my book group. Maybe I fear they share my initial image of him as the Liberace Vegas, drug-addled, kinky, gun-toting, bloated horror-show of the seventies. What if they respond like Claudia did?

I also see that cultural hero or Krishna though he may be, my Elvis-embarrassment lingers. I find myself skulking around record stores late at night, when I'm not likely to run into anyone I know. One evening I'm at the almost empty library with a few homeless men and some pimply teenagers probably working on summer school term papers. I find the Elvis books in the music section. He must have a lot of fans in Madison because two shelves are devoted to him. I select as many books as I can carry and take them to the check-out counter.

The librarian looks at them—*Dead Elvis--Chronicle of a Cultural Obsession, Mystery Train, Elvis and Me, Good Rocking Tonight, If I can Dream--The Spiritual Journey of Elvis Presley, Elvis and Gladys, Elvis Presley--Unseen Archives*— then at me, quizzically. I explain the books are for my adolescent niece who's just recently developed a crush on Elvis. "Anything to get her to read," I say blithely.

The profile of the typical Elvis fan—southern white woman, 35 to 55, with beehive hairdo, standing by her man who more often than not is a trucker—makes me distinctly uneasy. So does the description in *Elvis and You—Your Guide to the Pleasures of Being an Elvis Fan* of seriously overweight single women whose whole social life revolves around trips to Graceland and who plan to be buried with life-size Elvis dolls.

Maybe I need to admit to being "horrified." For now, I'm not ready to confess Elvis to my friends, but I'm not going to stop dancing.

If these Christians want me to believe in their god,

they'll have to sing me better songs...

I could only believe in a god that dances.

Nietzsche

4.

Gospel Elvis

By the middle of June, two weeks into my Elvis romance, I'm looking for something besides the Sun Sessions and the Gold album. Thumbing through the selections at Borders, I can't believe the number. Elvis has been dead 30 years! Country Elvis, Early Elvis, Vegas Elvis, Comeback Elvis, Movie Elvis, Balladeer Elvis, Elvis on Tour, Elvis from Hawaii, and four different albums of Gospel Elvis. Gospel Elvis? I had no idea he sang religious songs of the southern Pentecostal variety. I get the two-CD set, **Amazing Grace—His Most Sacred Performances**.

I put them on with no little trepidation. Talk about forbidden fruit. I'm the daughter of secular humanist Ph.D.s. My mother is an educator, my father an architect and professor of philosophy (specializing in logical positivism). My stepfather was an economist. All of them are in *Who's Who*. I like to think I get my intuitive right brain from the Navajos and my logical, intellectual left one from my parents. I should qualify that. My intellect is not the kind that wins prizes, excels at math, or belongs to Mensa. It's obsessed by those big questions that Allyn and I share. Anything to do with those I can be smart about.

My father disagrees. His comments about my inner life are scathing. He thinks I've wasted my brains messing around with "the stuff you B.S. about in college but wise–up to when you grow up and don't need a spiritual blankie to get you through the night." His dismissal of almost anything I hold dear is one of the many reasons I haven't seen him in years. I felt lucky to find Allyn, who didn't discount my search, and yet hadn't gone off some spiritual deep end that rejected science and reason.

I've also inherited something of my parent's highbrow tastes. Like them, I associate white gospel with an unsavory southern stew of hillbillies, the Klan, and the Scopes trial. For now, Elvis is bad enough. But Elvis singing Holy Roller hymns? My problem isn't so much the music, but the theology that goes with it. Gospel is pure Evangelical Christianity, which in my own opinionated way I define as: creationism, blood atonement and a punishing father whose own son has to die a hideous, excruciating death for our sins; a heaven out in space the Hubble never saw with a sinful earth just one step from hell; and the Rapture followed by a gory Second Coming, where Jesus literally falls out of the sky with sword in hand ready to smite the wicked.

Not that I'm not into Jesus. Since childhood, despite my agnostic parents, I've had an intimate relationship with Him. My mother tells a story of six-year-old me running out into the living room in my nightgown as their friends castigated religion late into the night. "Stop talking about Jesus that way!" I shouted. "He is one of my favorite relatives." When I was eight, my grandfather gave me a children's New Testament. I had just finished reading all the *Biographies for Young Readers* series, from George Washington to Winston Churchill. Jesus was something entirely different. His kindness to outcasts and women and his strange parables about prodigal sons and mustard seeds captured my imagination. Secretly, I acted out all the stories from the nativity to Pentecost, the door to my room closed. I dressed as Mary with a blue towel over my head, and as the Magdalene with a white one. This wasn't unusual behavior for me. My parents were busy getting degrees and working, so I spent a lot of time by myself in my room or wandering outdoors.

I developed a series of schoolgirl crushes on people whose lives I imagined imitated Jesus'. The first was on Father Damien, a Jesuit priest who chose to live with lepers and later died of leprosy himself. I read his biography, **Who Walk Alone,** over and over. My science fair projects for the next three years were all on leprosy. I was still acting out my fantasies behind closed doors. Wrapped in a sheet I thought made me look like Audrey Hepburn in *The Nun's Story*, I would pretend I was with Father Damien healing the lepers with my tears. Even then I was wearing lipstick. I thought a nun should be beautiful as well as good.

I went on to obsessions with Albert Schweitzer, Abraham Lincoln, and later Dorothy Day and Martin Luther King. In my mind, their Jesus cared for the poor and downtrodden. "Feed my lambs; clothe my sheep!" "As you do to the least of these, you have done to me." Jesus never denied the body. In the Gospel of Mark, the Pharisees described him as a "glutton and drunkard" who hung out with loose women, lepers, and outcasts.

By my junior year in high school, I had my own theology, a strange mix of Navajo Hozcho and Jesus. I believed that God was not a person, but an unfathomable something that not only created us and the world, but lived in us the way the Yeis did. We were like Jesus when we "walked in beauty" with each other and the earth. I could articulate this vision, and did—to a small group of girlfriends who thought I was the smartest, wisest person they knew. Secretly, I felt like a fraud. I could talk a good line but I was full of fear and self-doubt. I didn't have the faintest idea how to love myself or anybody else Jesus-style.

Over the next thirty years, I discovered many others who had gone before me and knew a lot more about the talk and how to walk it. I saw my small vision reflected in the big visions of Paul Tillich, Teilhard De Chardin, and Christian mystics like Meister Eckert, Thomas Merton and Simone Weil. From their perspective, the word *God* is a metaphor for something ineffable and unnamable. The world is the incarnation of this mystery and everything in it is sacred. The second coming happens when the Christ spirit rises in all our hearts, as it did in the man Jesus'.

I don't have a clue what Elvis would have thought about any of this, but after my Quaker vision I'm not ruling anything out. As far as his gospel music goes, all bad things are made good in the listening. Hearing Elvis sing gospel is like hearing Elvis come home to himself. His emotional range astounds me. He knows all the valleys and mountaintops of the spiritual life from longing to awe to surrender. The words are secondary. Elvis specializes in feeling. It is his native tongue.

He brings to gospel singing all the musical qualities that classical musician and university professor Charles T. Brown ascribed to him in his textbook, *The Art of Rock and Roll*. "Elvis had complete control of every aspect of vibrato…coupled with perfect pitch and an almost three-octave range….His ability to close his glottal flap and thereby stop a single note in its tracks was reputed to make women faint." His close friend, Joe Esposito, writes, "Few people grasped the quality of his passion and his ear. He was very, very particular about production, recording a song many times until he got exactly what he was hearing in his head."

One afternoon, I force my book-group friend, Odessa, who is a real gospel purist, to listen to him. We sit on her couch. She is tall and birdlike with flowing hair and an otherworldly air. Odessa closes her eyes and sways slightly. When the music stops, she is quite beside herself, calling Elvis's music "Uber Gospel." I ask her what she means. "Well, he makes every other singer feel forced, you know, like they're trying too hard to be spiritual." Odessa wonders why Elvis sounds so genuine, so in tune with the mystery.

Maybe it's because, as all Elvis's biographers agree, his roots are sunk in gospel. He once remarked unself-consciously, "My first love is spiritual music—some of those old colored spirituals from way back. I know practically every religious song ever written."

Elvis's knowing started young. His mother, Gladys Love Presley, had the kind of dirt-grinding life that longs for the sweetness of heaven. She was a devout churchgoer. Gladys described baby Elvis wiggling in her arms at church to the music. At age two, he ran up to join the singers, shaking his little body and humming along.

When he was eleven, Elvis discovered a black church frequented by sharecroppers a couple of miles outside of Tupelo, near the cotton fields. He convinced his cousin, Alan Greenwood, to come along with him every Sunday. They always went after white church and didn't tell anyone. Greenwood describes the first time he heard the music with Elvis. "He closed his eyes, moved to the rhythms and told me with complete authority, 'This is the way music is supposed t' be, comin' from deep down.'"

I read a story about Elvis's producers at RCA that delights me. Elvis always sang gospel to warm up before shows or recording sessions. The producers tried to get him to stop wasting his precious studio time and theirs "fooling around with gospel" until they realized he couldn't get the Elvis sound without it.

For the next two weeks, Elvis orchestrates my own personal revival meeting. Singing gospel, his voice is so sweet—utterly beautiful just like him. And he hasn't lost the beat for a second. His gospel dances me every bit as much as his rock 'n' romance. Day and night, I play Elvis gospel, clapping and shouting like a one-woman Pentecostal band. Nothing but exultation and joy. I follow Elvis straight to heaven.

Ritual dance and music provide a religious experience

more satisfying and convincing than any other.

It is with their muscles that humans

most easily attain knowledge of the divine.

Aldous Huxley

5.

Saturday Night and Sunday Morning

The summer solstice has come and gone, but Elvis and I are as hot as ever. Dancing to his gospel music, I wonder why it feels so sexy, so unlike any other Protestant hymns I've ever heard. I get a clue from a collection of readings for Claudia's African dance course that I find on our kitchen table. Her particular interest is in the African sources of African-American and Brazilian dance and music. She's been to Africa to do research many times, once on a Fulbright. I flip through the readings and discover an article, "Let That Long Snake Moan" by Michael Ventura, who explains that the difference between gospel and Protestant hymns is in their source.

The hymns come from Europe, straight through the Puritans and their terror of the fallen body cursed by original sin—better put a lid on sex, music, dance, and enjoyment, or God will fry your wicked body in hell forever. Southern gospel, black or white, comes from Africa via the slaves. Through all the horrors of slavery, African-Americans kept the essence of their old religion alive. In the African religion, heaven and earth are not separated by time and space. Rhythm and dance bring the spirit into the body. The body is the crossroads that unites the human and the divine.

Protestant hymns don't have a rock 'n' roll beat. The congregation is not supposed to get up and clap. Heaven forbid that someone should get ecstatic and out of hand in their sin-filled body! Gospel songs shout and holler, weep and moan, reveling in joy, exultation, longing, repentance, and salvation. They bypass the head, touch the heart, and grab the body. You want to clap your hands and stomp your feet. They are shockingly pleasurable. And shockingly personal. They're all about Jesus and how much he loves us. We need not fear his judgment. "Softly and sweetly Jesus is calling, calling you to come home."

Critics say the wild exuberant sound of early rock 'n' roll more closely resembles gospel than it does the sophisticated rhythms and heavy emotions of the blues. Elvis and all the early rockers, black and white, were churched. Rock 'n' roll is gospel's love child. No wonder listening to Elvis lifts me so.

And if elation isn't enough, there is also rejuvenation and healing. In between counseling sessions, instead of taking a nap, I put on the gospel and feel my cells jump to life, shot through with light. Years of neck tension and shoulder pain evaporate. A laying on of song, just like I witnessed as a child. Navajo medicine men are called "Singers" and their ceremonies "Sings" or "Chantways" because they heal through song. They believe singing vibrates their breath in a certain way that creates energetic healing. I tell this to Malynn, my physician friend. She patiently explains that moving to music with a rock beat releases feel-good endorphins, those internally generated opiates. Well, maybe—but I don't have the slightest doubt that Elvis knew something about the body and spirit that most of us don't.

His musical imagination and kinesthetic genius, fed by the rhythm and the beat, transcend boundaries and take us with him. Unlike many of his peers (Al Green, Jerry Lee Lewis, Little Richard) for whom "church" and "street" were inseparable divides, Elvis didn't seem to have any trouble mixing up body and spirit. He moved effortlessly from gospel to rock in every performance.

I read that in one of his early concerts in a school gym, he stunned the jitterbugging teens by suddenly launching into "Silent Night." Watching the "Comeback Special" for the fourth time, I notice again that the gospel section is followed by a bordello scene where Elvis enjoins his leggy lovely to "take it real easy, relax, and let yourself go." In the "Elvis on Tour" video, the no-holds-barred "How Great Thou Art" elicits as much audience hysteria as the love songs. Elvis stops in the midst of a concert to invite J. D. Sumner and the Stamps to sing "There Is a Sweet, Sweet Spirit in This Place." Elvis becomes absolutely still; even the audience falls silent. Then he swings right into "Lawdy Mizz Clawdy," followed by a Ray Charles tune.

Elvis was such a fan of Charles's own intuitive blending of gospel and blues that he included "I Got a Woman" on his 1956 debut album. Secular and sacred, sexual and spiritual, all fit into a comfortable whole. I get a full-blown epiphany about this, complete with goose bumps, watching Martin Scorsese's documentary about African-American blues singers. In it, musician Bobby Rush says, "My woman lifts me up on Saturday night, same way Jesus does Sunday morning." Scorsese keeps shaking his head. He grew up Catholic; no wonder he doesn't get it. But I do. For Elvis, like Rush, Saturday night and Sunday morning are in the same time zone.

I spend my morning walks ruminating about Saturday night and Sunday morning. One's a date with dancing and music, pleasure and sex. The other's an appointment with spirit. If you put them in the same time zone, do you get heaven on earth? What happens to Saturday night when it denies spirit, and to Sunday morning when it denies the body? Does pleasure become addictive and self-absorbed? Does religion become life-denying and puritanical?

I barely notice the trees or anything else as I walk. I wonder how Saturday night and Sunday morning got separated in the first place. Why did the early Greeks and the Africans think dancing and music and sex wake up the spirit in the body? Why don't Christians and Buddhists think that? What would happen if sex was soulful and pleasure sanctified?

Can Elvis really sing me whole? Eighty million fans world-wide all agree he's Mr. Saturday Night. But is he Mr. Sunday Morning too? Sure he sang gospel, but did he have a good heart?

I discover the answer in all those Elvis biographies I've been plowing through. The reason Elvis sounds so sincere singing gospel is that he was. In his own mind he was someone who tried to be a good Christian. He said to his spiritual friend and guide, Larry Geller, "All good things come from God. You don't have to go to church. Sure church helps, but you can be a Christian so long as you have a Christian heart." After the release of his album, "Walk a Mile in My Shoes," Elvis said: "If you hate another human being you are hating a part of yourself...God is a living presence in all of us."

Elvis identified passionately with underdogs and children. He wasn't fooling when he sang of a better land "where all my brothers walk hand in hand," or about our responsibility for a child who becomes an angry young man and is killed "in the ghetto." He recorded both songs—over the strenuous objection of his domineering manager, the infamous Colonel Parker—in response to Martin Luther King's assassination.

And he didn't just sing his compassion. Elvis was a giver, too. He made four billion dollars and gave away two billion. The Elvis Presley Charitable Foundation paid the medical bills for thousands of seriously ill children whose parents couldn't afford to. Even in his last drugged-out years, when he rarely took calls from anyone, he always took them from parents with sick children. In 1970, in honor of his philanthropy, Elvis was given the U.S. Jaycees award as one of the nation's ten outstanding young men. In his acceptance speech, he said of his fellow nominees, "See, these are the type of people who care. They're dedicated. You realize they might be building the kingdom of heaven right here." The award was so important to him that he carried it with him on tour or on vacation.

It's such a relief to find so much goodness in Elvis, because there's no mistaking: I'm spending way too much time with this guy! As I read about him, I've taken to writing down pertinent points on note cards. I organize the cards by topics like charity, compassion, intelligence, spirituality (with a Saturday night/Sunday morning subsection). All this effort is inspired by a funny dream I have near the end of June:

> *I'm in the Bill O'Reilly "No Spin Zone." He's using me as an excuse to rant about Elvis as the evil instigator of the sixties, responsible for all the current sexual excess, unwed mothers, and abortions. I can't get a word in edgewise, but I have a file box full of the kind of 3-by-5 inch note cards I used as a debater. I*

aim it at O'Reilly's heart. Minute by minute, he starts to shrink. Finally, he's only about three inches high, but he's still waving his arms and ranting in a high squeaky voice.

I wake up laughing. It occurs to me that if I'm going to convince my friends I haven't gone completely mad, I'd better be able to defend Elvis. Note cards feel like just the way to go. My desk looks like command central for Operation Redemption Elvis. It's piled with Elvis books and articles. (Google *Elvis* and get 4.3 million hits in one third of a second!) I have so many note cards waiting to be filed they're spilling onto the floor. You'd think I was writing a Ph.D. thesis.

I leave two of my June entries from my *Elvis and Race* card-file section on the kitchen table for Claudia, who's convinced Elvis is a racist. Card one reads:

On tour, Elvis always had black musicians like Myrna Smith of the Sweet Inspirations on stage with him. At the Astrodome in Texas, the promoters told him, "You can leave the black girls home." Elvis demanded the full star treatment for them, saying, "You don't like it, deal with it, or I'm not going to be there." When Jerry Schilling, one of the Memphis mafia, wanted to move in with Myrna, he was afraid of the effect on the fans and the other guys. Elvis simply said, "You're my friend, Myrna's my friend, and you are both always welcome at my home."

The second card reads:

In a 1956 interview, Elvis said, "The colored folks been singing it and playing it like I'm doing now, man, for more years than I know...nobody paid it no mind till I goosed it up. I got it from them. I used to hear old Arthur Crudup bang his box the way I do now and I said if I ever got to the place where I could feel all old Arthur felt, I'd be a music man like nobody ever saw."

On the bottom, I leave Claudia a P.S. "Guess what James Brown said about Elvis?—'I wasn't just a fan, he was my brother. He said I was good and I said he was good. We never argued about that. There'll never be another like that soul brother.'"

I'm determined to convince Claudia that Elvis really was a good guy. Despite my lingering shame, the more I get to know him, the less ashamed I feel. He works in my heart in mysterious ways. I'm thinking about those fans I read about who horrified me just a few weeks ago. They've always known Elvis is magic, and now I do, too.

****

Our July book group gathering is at Odessa's house. The evening is hot and sweaty. The mosquitoes are gigantic and ferocious, as if they've mated with Bengal tigers, so we sit inside. Odessa takes sustainability seriously, and there's no air conditioning. The table is set for summer: fresh flowers, linen napkins embroidered with wood violets, and cold foods—an asparagus quiche, wild mushroom strudel, bowls of strawberries, and an iced sweet German wine.

When we sit down to eat at nine, it's still light. We hardly speak except to make happy food noises; it's all so good. When we get to the strawberries and cream, Harvey asks, "So what's new with Elvis?"

"Something very, very big," I say, trying to imitate Ed Sullivan, whom I've seen a lot of recently while watching early Elvis film clips. "Elvis puts Saturday night and Sunday morning in the same time zone."

"Oh, I like that," Harvey murmurs. "Church and 'street' brought together in the beat."

Hedda looks at us skeptically. Sitting down, Hedda appears voluptuous and dreamy, her green eyes open and vulnerable to every impression. Standing up, she's short and rounded like a Ukrainian peasant. She's an unusual combination of artistic and intuitive, earthy and practical. "I don't get it," she says. "What do Saturday night and Sunday morning even refer to?"

Her question is my opening. I launch into the ideas that have come to me in my walks. Elvis, I tell them, is just like us. Somehow he knew what everyone else forgot—you can pray with your body. You don't have to settle for being spiritual or sexual. Singing and dancing and sex can bring you as close to God and to the God in each other as prayer or good works. I'm just getting into a groove when Odessa comes up behind me. Very gently she puts one hand over my mouth. "No more talking Elvis to death," she whispers. With the other hand she pushes the CD play button. "Time for Elvis Yoga!" she shouts, clapping and shaking her hips.

The gospel anthem, "I Got a Feeling in My Body," fills the room with a driving rock 'n' roll beat, and we're all on our feet, clapping and swaying. Harvey grabs both my hands, pulls me close, pushes back and twirls me around. Margaret and Hedda, Odessa and Malynn partner up, too. The CD blasts out one danceable gospel tune after another and we rock away, as if Jesus himself was hosting American Bandstand.

He had something at once physical and mystical

that put him in the realm of the beyond,

far beyond any of his contemporaries....

The only credible explanation is that

Elvis was from another planet, like Superman

or someone in the Old Testament.

Lester Bangs

6.
Elvis Christ

The "dog days" have arrived. Madison in July is as steamy as the tropics; the temperature and humidity can reach ninety-nine. The heat feels appropriate. It doesn't seem possible, but I've made a discovery that brings my Elvis romance to a new boiling point. Elvis was as much of a reader and seeker as I am—every bit as disenthralled with organized religion, but just as spiritual. Here I am with three university degrees and Elvis had barely graduated from high school, yet we had read the same authors from Aldous Huxley and Timothy Leary to Yogananda and Herman Hesse!

My first inklings of Elvis's unusual spiritual interests come to me on a bright July morning at Borders as I'm browsing through the Elvis books. ***Elvis Day by Day*** exhaustively highlights each day of his life. On page seventy-two is a photo from Elvis's own copy of ***The Secret Doctrine***, a dense theosophical text that I have also read. Elvis has underlined this sentence: "The world of form is created through sound vibrations." In the margin he's written, "God loves me best when I sing." I can't believe it. Elvis the sexy gospel singer just wouldn't be enough for me over the long haul, but Elvis the sexy spiritual seeker will.

Elvis and Gladys shared a living Pentecostal faith. She believed Elvis's dead twin Jesse watched over them and could be called upon for help. They spoke with Jesse and Jesus daily. In their two-room Tupelo shack, the whole family prayed together every night on their knees. His mother's death in 1958 must have socked Elvis's naive faith in the belly. How could a just God have taken her at the moment he was finally making her life good? On her tombstone he defiantly wrote, "Your will, not mine." And then there was the matter of his fame: Why had he been chosen? What was God's will for him, his life purpose? And why, despite all his money, adulation, and endless pleasures, wasn't he happy? He confided to a preacher, "What you're lookin' at is the unhappiest young man on earth!"

In the popular mind, he might have been the consummate party boy, but all my reading points towards a man haunted by faith. Everything needed to be squared with God. He even rationalized his sleeping around (before and during his marriage to Priscilla) as the prerogative of King David and King Solomon and, therefore, okay for him. Books became Elvis's first clue that there might be more to faith than fundamentalism. In 1956, June Jaunico, an early girlfriend, gave him Kahlil Gibran's *The Prophet*. Elvis devoured the philosophy of the book, memorizing whole pages that he could recite at will. As with all the other spiritual books he treasured, he gave away thousands of copies. June's gift was always by his bedside at Graceland, or on tour with him, until he died.

The Prophet could be described as mysticism for beginners. It offered a way of thinking that Elvis had never been exposed to before. Fundamentalism rejects the sinful body and the fallen earth, but offers the promise of heaven if, as one of Elvis's gospel sideman put it, "we're good little boys and girls." Gibran writes that the earth is the face of God, and we are his body.

It's hard for me to imagine the twenty-year-old Elvis who horrified preachers and parents reading, much less memorizing, **The Prophet.** The standard rap on Elvis was, and is, that he was an ignorant southern bubba. Even Lester Bangs, the New York music critic who believed that Elvis's looks and talent so far exceeded anyone else's that he must be from another planet, refers to him as "a big dumb hillbilly with an IQ only a few points above his mule." I love discovering stories that blow the stereotype. I gobble up Peter Guralnick's painstakingly researched books that set the gold standard in Elvis biography, **Last Train to Memphis** and **Careless Love.**

My favorite story that I recount to Claudia immediately is about Billy Goldberg and Elvis. Billy was a Broadway composer and Columbia graduate who helped produce the Comeback Special. He didn't think much of Elvis as a person or a musician when he was hired. But the first time he encountered Elvis, Elvis was by himself trying to play parts of Beethoven's "Moonlight Sonata" by ear. He asked Billy if he knew the piece and to show him the rest. "I was so surprised. But he was an incredibly quick study…He has class. Underneath all that stuff, suddenly I found someone I could relate to."

Elvis's serious reading—we're talking about more than a thousand books—began when he met Larry Geller on a movie set in 1960. This meeting was so over-the-top it seems almost apocryphal. Geller was a hairdresser, one of the most sought after in Hollywood; but by calling, he was a spiritual seeker and teacher. Elvis immediately asked Geller what was important to him. Geller said that the central questions of his own meditation and his work with others were, "Where do we come from? Why are we here? What is our life purpose?" "Man, I have been waiting for you all my life," Elvis enthused. "I'm asking myself these questions all the time."

Peter Guralnick writes: For the next four hours he was like a parched man in the desert: he bared his entire soul. He told Larry all the things he secretly thought and could share with no one around him. "Man, Larry," he said, "I swear to God no one knows how lonely I get. And how empty I really feel."

The next day Geller, now officially employed by Elvis, arrived on the set with the ***The Autobiography of a Yogi*** by Paramahansa Yogananda, a Hindu holy man who brought Vedantic mysticism to California. Elvis devoured the book and told Geller, "Man, keep on bringing me those kinda books." For the next two years, the two men were seldom apart. Geller went back and forth with him from Hollywood to Graceland, presiding over Elvis's spiritual education.

Elvis kept Larry close, despite the veiled anti-Semitism of the Memphis Mafia (the nickname for his entourage), as well as Priscilla and the Colonel. They called Larry "the wandering Jew." Elvis' response was to carve a Star of David on his mother's tombstone and to make the Memphis Mafia wear watches that alternately flashed a Star of David and a cross. Much to his daddy Vernon's alarm, Elvis delightedly broadcast a long-hidden family secret: one of Gladys's close kin was Jewish.

Larry brought Elvis hundreds of books. Elvis read them, memorized and underlined important passages, and covered the pages with his own notes. Larry taught Elvis how to meditate and brought him to see his own teacher, Sri Daya Mata, Yogananda's spiritual successor at The Self-Realization Fellowship Center outside of Hollywood. Elvis was so drawn to her that he considered becoming a monk. She told him his gift was song and to keep on singing. Still, he spent hours in the Center's meditation garden and built a smaller version at Graceland, complete with lotus fountain.

Learning all this, I have to keep pinching myself. Elvis could have been reading anything from girlie magazines to westerns. Instead, he was meditating and reading most of the same spiritual books I have. The book that seems to have had the most profound effect on Elvis was ***The Impersonal life,*** written by Joseph Brenner in 1917. Little is known about Brenner except that he was an American and a non-denominational Christian. His ability to translate mystical principles into a Christian idiom probably appealed to Elvis's own roots and sensibilities. Brenner's style is weird—annoyingly archaic and bombastic—but his message is startling. He asserts that Jesus was a man, a channel for Christ consciousness. He is the son of God only to the extent that we are all sons and daughters of God. Brenner insists that we are literally cells in the body of God manifesting in the world of form. More radical is his insistence that heaven is on earth, but only when all men become channels for the same Christ consciousness that Jesus expressed in his life and being.

Elvis took Brenner's message literally. He confided to Larry that he had a special mission: to spread Jesus' message of love through his singing. ***The Impersonal Life*** was so important to Elvis that he passed out copies to all the people on his movie sets and in his bands, to family and friends, and to every new girlfriend. Over his lifetime, he gave away thousands.

Five years after the millennium we are so awash in New Age mysticism, from Deepak Chopra to Eckhart Tolle, that **The Impersonal Life** seems almost ho-hum. But America in the fifties? It's hard to fathom what Hollywood or Elvis's peers must have thought. To unbelievers the book must have seemed pure gibberish; to believers, pure blasphemy.

Of all Elvis's books, **The Impersonal Life** interests me the most. I had never heard of it, or Brenner, yet the message mirrors many of my own spiritual views. In early July, my Elvis delirium reaches its pinnacle. I'm still wearing love blinders and not ready to ask the obvious question, "So why did he end so badly?" For most of the month, I walk on water in the place "where music and moonlight and feeling are one." True romance, just like the poet Shelley said. I leave my house in the morning humming Elvis, and I'm still humming when I return at the end of the day. In the evenings, Elvis and I dance.

Claudia finds my "Elvis thing" (as she calls it) ridiculous, despite my debate cards. She says, "It just doesn't make sense for someone to be so happy for nothing."

"It's not nothing, I'm in love!"

The allure of Elvis continues to escape her until the day she comes home unexpectedly as the gospel's blasting. I invite her into my room and make her listen to some of the early rockers, too. After an hour, she says thoughtfully, "You know, in African music, it's the singer, not the drums, like you might think, who charges the atmosphere and brings the spirit into the circle. The song carries the heart." She looks at me in a dreamy way. "That Elvis, his voice is so achingly pure, like sweet waters on those gospel songs, and so sexy and joyous on the others. He really *is* the King." I touch her arm and smile. We're having a perfect Elvis moment. I know it won't last; Claudia's moods are like chameleons. Later, when she leaves to go dancing, she says a little bashfully, "Now, about Elvis being the king…"

Whatever Claudia thinks, I can't wait to tell all my other friends about this great guy I've fallen for and how they can, too. I ask my friend, Tom, who does professional audio work, to put together my personal top ten: "Baby Let's Play House," "Mystery Train," "You'll Never Walk Alone," "Way Down," "Only Believe," "Big Hunk of Love," "Milk Cow Boogie," "Bridge Over Troubled Water," "It Hurts Me," and "If I Can Dream." I decide to have Elvis parties every

Thursday afternoon with my friends, one friend at a time.

I prepare my room by bringing in great bundles of pink and white roses. I'm going to serve sweet iced tea (an Elvis favorite), but decide against another favorite—peanut butter and fried banana sandwiches. Claudia calls my room "the shrine." It is a twenty by ten foot rectangle, with a bank of windows and hanging plants on the very long west side. Nine yards of lace hang from the ceiling to the floor like waterfall. All the furniture is low to the ground Japanese style, except for three floor-to-ceiling bookcases. My computer workstation and file cabinets are hidden behind a bamboo and rice paper screen. During the day my bed becomes a couch. On a low table in front of it sit a carved wooden Buddha and a statue of St. Francis holding a small black Madonna.

Jean is my first guinea pig. She's a radio talk show host and poet who has spent most of her life trying to reconcile her desire to be a nun *and* a sexy, rock 'n' roll rebel. Jean's a Catholic, so this is about as impossible as squaring the circle. Her outfit reflects her contradictions—demure pearl earrings that complement her huge almond eyes and dark hair, a soft muslin shirt buttoned at the neck, a blue miniskirt, and faux alligator boots. I start by sharing my Quaker vision and telling her about Saturday night and Sunday morning. Then I show her the Krishna montage and Elvis's reading list. That's all the foreplay she needs. Now we're ready to dance. First, I play "You'll Never Walk Alone," and gradually work my way through the ballads to the shake-the-rafter rockers, ending with "Way Down": "Way down where the healing lays/ way down where the music plays." Elvis is utterly irresistible. Jean and I shimmy like lap dancers and sway like choir-robed "Born Agains." It may be Thursday afternoon, but Saturday night and Sunday morning have come to town. "Lord have mercy!"

    The next week my friend Diana, arrives unexpectedly from New York. She's come to Madison to see her brother. Forty years ago, she was designated by Mayor Koch as "New York's official storyteller," and she still tells stories in Central Park as well as all around the world. Diana, dressed in layers of elegant ethnic clothing, looks like a modest Scherazade. I serve her sweet iced tea along with my Elvis spiel and invite her to dance. She's hesitant, but totally intrigued by Elvis's spiritual side. "I can't believe he gave so much money away," she says approvingly. "I was scared of Elvis when I first heard him," she continues. "I was thirteen;

he was too sexy, too dangerous." I start slow with the ballads. By the time I get to "Let's Play House," all her shirts, skirts and vests are flying about her slender body. "Oh you must give me this CD, I really need to do more grinding. I forget to dance," she gasps, flopping down on my couch.

One by one, all of my friends succumb to Elvis. His voice falls on them, just like it does on me, with a great big Molly Bloom "Yes!" They share long-forgotten Elvis memories. Jean, who grew up in a Catholic household where sex was strictly taboo, says she had a big Elvis poster hidden in her closet. "He was my first heartthrob." Hedda even describes her own mini-Elvis-miracle in a Memphis hotel at a lawyer's convention. She'd had a migraine and gone upstairs to rest. She dreamed Elvis came to the foot of her bed, dressed all in white and with a white guitar, and sang to her. She woke up headache-free and went downstairs where she was astonished to find the dining room decorated with Elvis memorabilia. It was the second anniversary of his death.

They try to say what you are, spiritual or sexual?

They wonder about King Solomon and all his wives…

But we have ways within each other

that will never be said by anyone.

Rumi

7.
That Many-Splendored Thing

It's the middle of July. Just six weeks since my Quaker vision and I'm still head over heels crazy about Elvis. I've never felt so alive. I'm totally in this moment, here and now. When I listen to him or dance, I stop thinking about the past or the future. I'm fully in my body. It's like I've come to my senses—alive to sound, sight, and feeling. Elvis reminds me of how erotic I felt as a child. Before school grabbed hold of me and I lost that full-bodied joy, sex was all around—in the apple trees, the ants making their little hogans, the warm dirt, the smell of tortillas and the taste of peaches.

Now Elvis wakes my whole body up. Nothing but delight and all the goodwill Beethoven's chorus praises in the "Ode to Joy": "Joy, divine spark of the Gods/ your magic reunites what custom has parted/ all men become brothers where your gentle wings rest." Touched by joy, the entire world is my intimate friend. I'm in love with the bank tellers, my clients, the trees, the clouds.

Of course, I'm mainly in love with Elvis. I try to get a fix on the whys of my obsession. Somehow, I feel that Elvis understands me in a way no man ever has. He dances effortlessly with so many of the contradictions I find in myself. His own are on full display in "The Comeback Special." Shouting out the rockers and moving his hips, Elvis is raunchy, but never sleazy—a dangerous black-leather-clad Adonis who's also a sweet kid having a whole lot of fun. He sings gospel songs and the quiet ballad, "Memories" perfectly straight without irony. In the midst of a set change, he thrusts his mike stand at the audience shouting, "Moby Dick!" The gesture is both humorous and audacious, as if he knows those fans are also his white whale. A minute later he makes fun of his early love songs and his curling lip—"You remember this lip: it starred in 29 films." A serious statement about the origins of rock and roll in gospel and rhythm and blues follows. Elvis contains multitudes.

I love the way Elvis redefined masculinity—he wasn't a "suit" or a Marlboro Man. There's something so feminine about him. He was tender-faced, pretty, drawn to bright colors and sensuous clothes. In his music, body and soul meet and greet. Sexy, beautiful Elvis ("gyrating like a woman," as one critic sniffed) sings to me like a Greek priestess celebrating the women's mysteries at Eleusis. At the same time, this is a seriously macho guy. Forget the vestal virgins. There isn't anyone he wants but you.

When I listen to Elvis, I'm not hearing an unattainable star or a dead man. He is right there in the room with me. How can this be? I get a clue from the writer, Michael Ventura. He claims that Elvis's music, more than any other singer's, is directly connected to his body. Even when he recorded gospel by himself, he moved. Elvis once joked, "When you got rhythm, man, you got it all over." Encoded in each note is his movement. When I listen, I take in his voice and his body. No wonder there are so many Elvis sightings! His music brings him to life. Or maybe it's that there's so much life in his life, you just can't imagine him dead.

I feel he tunes directly, beeline-straight, into my heart, without any calculation or manipulation. I think this has something to do with his relationship with Gladys. The death of Elvis's twin brother in childbirth created an unusually intense bond between Elvis and his mother. In photos they are always a twosome with daddy Vernon either absent or hovering in the background. Elvis has his arms around Gladys, always touching her in some way, while they whisper their own private language of baby talk and endearments.

Gladys's troubles and fears became his, as did her dreams of fame and fortune. From early on, Elvis's mission was to use his glorious voice to bootstrap his "babies," as he called both Vernon and Gladys, out of destitution. He said of Gladys's early death, "The bottom dropped out of my life the day she died. I felt I had nothing left. In a way I was right. Everything I did was for her." In turn, she doted on him shamelessly. Even in his twenties, she was still feeding him his favorite peanut butter and banana sandwiches by hand and brushing away the crumbs. I imagine Elvis loves me flat-out, the way he did her. He's going to make love to me right now *and* he will cherish and protect me in every way forever.

There is something else: every other time I've been in love, even with Allyn, I've felt self-conscious. My love feelings get muddied by my fearful ones. I'm afraid of the other's judgment. I worry about looking good. Aging hasn't helped. My feminist and spiritual selves are appalled, but that's the way it is. My mother insists that it's what's inside that counts, but I can't dismiss beauty so easily. "The eyes," as the troubadours noted some five hundred years ago, "are the scouts of the heart."

Elvis can't see me, so I can relax in a way I never have. The effect of this is startling: not being the direct object of Elvis's desire, I can more deeply feel my own. The sound of his intake of breath on a song sets my heart racing. I love to look at him. The perfection of his profile and impossibly thick lashes, the glow of his skin and broad shoulders fill me with happy excitement, as if I've just received the best possible news. Elvis is a fire that burns through me without burning. He's warm and gives off light. The whole world glows. "Hot flashes," says Claudia.

"Love," I counter. I find myself flirting with everyone and everything. An encounter with a cup of jasmine tea has overtones of a love affair. I inhale its voluptuous aroma, feel the heat of the warm cup through every finger and let the hot tea enter my mouth like a French kiss.

Harvey comes up to my room for an Elvis Thursday. Elvis is so seductive. We slow dance enveloped by his musical come-on. The gospel carries an even more erotic charge. I'm walking a fine line here.

Am I going to start making love with all my friends as well as cups of tea? When he leaves, Harvey touches my face. "You look like a Botticelli Venus." It's probably the light, but I certainly feel that way.

When Allyn comes back to Madison for a week, he has a different take. After listening to me prattle on about Elvis and sing gospel all week long, he tells me I look possessed. Allyn isn't concerned about Elvis. Elvis is dead. He's concerned about me. Before he leaves for his cottage again, he says, "Willow, don't mistake the finger for the moon. You think you're in love with Elvis, what you're really in love with is what he represents and how he makes you feel." Allyn doesn't ask, "How is that different from what I represent and how I make you feel?" But I need to ask.

****

I'm on one of my morning walks and thinking about my relationship to the two men in my life. Elvis and me—that's pretty straightforward. I walk through the doorway of Elvis right into my own ecstatic joy. Images of Allyn over our seventeen years together come to me. Allyn, like Elvis, is easy on the eyes. His aquiline nose and curvy lips, even his build remind me of Elvis. It occurs to me that he is what Elvis would have been like if he'd grown old well. When Allyn and I first started dating, Odessa referred to him as "the dreamboat." He seemed to be surrounded by a number of women who thought he was a dreamboat and a guru. When I asked about them, he laughed. "Those are my friends, and if anyone treats me like a guru, I immediately start picking my nose." To be fair, he was also surrounded by a number of men. Babies and small children gaze at him in restaurants. In a roomful of people, any pet on the premises will seek him out.

    I described him to my mother as a cross between Jimmy Stewart and Merlin. He grew up in a small town in Michigan and has an "aw shucks, straight-arrow" quality. There is something about his height and silver hair and round owl eyes that invoke a feeling of wisdom and protection. A friend of mine who'd been his client before I knew him described Allyn as "an instant placebo effect. All you have to do is walk in his office and suddenly you know no matter how messed up you are, you're going to be okay."

    Someone said, "After forty you're responsible for your looks." The aura of wisdom and kindness Allyn evokes is honestly come by. He describes himself as "a born again Buddhist," but he doesn't buy into Buddhist dogma and rituals or guru worship. He describes religious beliefs as "loaded guns usually held to somebody else's head" and responsible for most of the violence in the world. What draws him to Buddhism is its emphasis on mindfulness, compassion, and genuine experience, rather than faith. Mindfulness is a way of becoming more and more aware of all the conditioned beliefs and emotional habits that keep you from living authentically and loving others.

I found mindfulness hard to grasp. It's not like ordinary thinking; it's more like seeing through your thinking. But I wanted to know what Allyn knew. From the time of our first meeting, I sensed that he lived the loving-kindness I only thought about. Our relationship has been a kind of hands-on curriculum in mindfulness, although Allyn hasn't treated me like his student. Mostly I've learned by watching him.

Early on, he did recommend some books he thought I might be interested in and showed me how to meditate. "Meditation," he said, "is not a big deal. It's just a way to develop your inner witness, then you can watch your emotions and thoughts without getting caught by them." He suggested that I could use meditation sessions to ask the "Who am I?" question. "Maybe the eye with which you see the mystery is the same eye with which it sees you," he said with a laugh.

Allyn's words may be hanging out there on a spiritual edge, but he isn't. His life is orderly and practical. He always turns out lights. He never ever wastes food. All his new clothes are from Goodwill and he still wears his clothes from high school. His closet, like the rest of his apartment, is organized with military precision. In the beginning, his neatness drove me crazy. Our first dinner together was on a spring evening. The apple trees had just bloomed. To mark both occasions, I made apple crepes sprinkled with confectioner's sugar. I scattered apple blossoms on the tablecloth and my red brick floor in the same spirit a Japanese cook marks the coming of the full moon by placing a round slice of white radish in everyone's bowl of soup. The next day Allyn presented me with a dust buster. Inwardly I suspected him of being a bit of an old maid, but his neatness seems to come from his respect for time and energy, and his dislike of waste.

There is an easy balance in his life. He walks to work every morning, stays until noon, spends a few hours working on his financial portfolio (psychotherapists don't get pensions, and he's set up trust funds for his two sons and grandchildren, as well as a philanthropy fund). In the evening he spends time with me, his family and friends, and reads science magazines or meditates. He loves movies and watching the news. I find the nonstop agony of the news disturbing, and asked why he didn't. He said that he liked seeing how we were doing as a species—"Think of the news as a kind of computer print-out of the human condition."

Despite our mutual belief that loving-kindness is the highest value, we have more serious differences. Allyn values simplicity and efficiency. For me, it's all about beauty. When I first accompanied him to Quaker meeting, I commented on the lack of beauty and color. "Quakers want to be simple," he said. "There is real beauty in simplicity. Think about Zen flower arranging."

"No," I countered, "it's deeply different. Quakers are drab because they're ascetics who don't want to be lured by beauty or tempted by the flesh. Those are distractions from God. Zen artists see beauty as revealing spirit in the world."

I wondered how much Quakerism and Buddhism had to do with Allyn's refusal to dance. From my point of view, both religions are deeply disrespectful of the body. For Quakers the body is fallen until it resurrects in heaven, for Buddhists it's a necessary illusion. I don't think of the fall as a fall at all. For me, the Mystery emerges in us, like the ocean emerges in the waves. Dancing and music are ways God expresses joy. With our bodies, we make spirit matter. Allyn prefers silence and he absolutely will not dance. "It's just not who I am," he insists. "You dance, I'll watch."

    When I challenged him about his own feelings about the body, he said, "Well, for me the body *is* just a temporary vehicle through which spirit passes, but my opposition to dancing can be laid fair and square at the door of Miss Gustafson and her School for the Dance. I had to go there every Saturday for ten years while all my buddies got to play hockey and fish."

    One day, I found a picture in a family album of a ten-year-old Allyn at a dance recital wearing a top hat and holding a cane. Cute little girls smile on either side, while Allyn grimaces. "My mother kept shouting 'Smile! Smile!' from the audience," he said when I showed him the photo. "The way I saw it, there wasn't a darn thing to smile about."

    When we walk together in the Arboretum, Allyn walks fast, never missing the forest for the trees. I like to dawdle over every spider web and trout lily. He's a Big Picture guy. He wants to know "what transpires behind what appears." I think God is in the details. It's as if we are looking at the same mystery through different lenses—his is a telescope and mine a magnifying glass. Allyn is seeking the source; I'm enthralled with all its manifestations. Our differences reminded me of a book I'd read on medieval male and female mystics. The author concluded that for men, self-transcendence involved dissolving into a luminous void; for women, losing the self catapulted them fully into the world. St. John of the Cross described a flaming light in the dark. Hildegard of Bingen saw a great tree with the five senses inscribed in gold on every branch.

    If Elvis is my doorway into ecstatic joy, Allyn is a doorway into wisdom. Although Allyn and Elvis occupy different places on the spiritual spectrum, spiritually they both point in the same direction. Elvis said he was "singing to bring Jesus' love into the world." Allyn would say that that is precisely the purpose of psychotherapy and mindfulness—to create the inner freedom that makes such love possible. But the more I think about what each represents, the more I realize I don't care. I'm not interested in a relationship with two metaphors; I just want to be with Allyn *and* with Elvis.

****

Claudia and I are sitting in her gazebo after her birthday extravaganza. It's almost eleven, way past my bedtime. The yard is covered with paper flowers. Motown tapes play in the background. The fireflies are flashing their lights at one another and still partying. The gazebo is screened so we don't have to fight with the mosquitoes, and we're having a brief respite from our usual sweaty summer nights. The air touches our skin so lightly it's hardly there. I ask Claudia, "Do you remember that book, **The Two Loves of Dona Flor**?"

"Oh, the one where the first husband dies and she lives with the second, but the other one makes love to her day and night from the spirit world?"

"Yeah, he's this great lover but a two-timing rascal, and the other one is a sensible druggist who adores her. Anyway, the author describes her as the happiest person in Brazil. That's kind of how I feel with Elvis and Allyn."

"Because Allyn is a sensible psychologist and Elvis is a sex maniac?" she asks incredulously. "There is something so weird about this, like you're having a guilt-free affair with a dead man." She emphasizes the word "dead."

"It's not like that at all, Claudia. They're both spiritual and sexy, just in different ways. Elvis—

Claudia interrupts me with her signature laugh—something halfway between a giggle and a snort. "You," she says "have had way, way too much wine."

I give her a look and go upstairs to bed. I don't want to discuss it with her, but I wonder if Claudia is on to something. Am I having a "guilt-free affair with a dead man?" I want to think my Elvis romance is about Quaker Meeting and that I'm learning something about love from him that I didn't from Allyn. When I feel Elvis joy, I don't have to try to be loving; I spontaneously feel one with everyone. Maybe I'm less subtle than Allyn, and that's why mindfulness practice doesn't fully work for me. Or, maybe, the practice laid the foundation and walls, and Elvis adds the roof.

But what if my love affair with Elvis isn't about that at all? Would I be doing Elvis if Allyn weren't away so much? If he were more romantic? Could I be playing out some version of Doris Lessing's novel, *The Summer Before the Dark,* in which a middle-aged woman seeks wild erotic satisfaction before old age closes all the doors? Then I have a really subversive thought: "Well, if that's the case, what a clever way to do it. I can have my Elvis and Allyn, too."

Then it occurs to me that I am doing what all those southern, beehive-haired women probably do—

make their relationship to their husbands better by placing their unfulfilled fantasies on Elvis. And not just those women. What about all the millions of screaming fans (male and female) who find some unlived part of themselves in Elvis? These thoughts ought to unsettle me but they don't. For once in my life I'm part of the crowd, and not sticking out like some over-intellectual, hyper-sensitive sore thumb.

And yet… My last thought as I drift off to sleep is that something about all this is very unfair to Allyn. If Elvis really is the key to that room of ecstatic delight, I need to share Elvis with Allyn.

Between the idea and the reality falls the shadow.

T. S. Eliot

8.
Almost Heartbreak Hotel

By the last week in July, the romance has soured. Too much information. I break up with Elvis every other day, disappointed and confused by one tawdry shocker after the next. The first was his blatant sexism. "Elvis's ideas about women were pre-Civil War," said Larry Geller. Although he was spellbinding, kind, humorous, considerate, a sensitive lover, and a great provider for all his women, he liked them young, virginal, and obedient. When asked what kind of women he was attracted to, Elvis said, "I like all kinds, you know, schoolgirls and starlets." Much later, drugged, lonely and impotent, he was asked by his buddies why he didn't go out with someone his own age—someone he could talk to.

Elvis asked, "What could a forty-two-year old woman do for me?" Instead he took up with Ginger Alden, a twenty-year-old Memphis beauty queen who reminded him of Gladys.

Virginity was essential. His cousin Alan Greenwood noted Elvis's alarm if "it was too loose down there." Heaven forbid you should have a baby. Elvis told a girl he was dating that a baby was "God's way of telling a woman she had a sacred responsibility, she isn't supposed to go around trying to be sexy." This meant he couldn't sleep with his own wife after the birth of his daughter.

None of his relationships seem to have been between two consenting adults on equal terms, nor to be ones of shared physical, intellectual and emotional intimacy. In the two years he spent with Elvis and Priscilla, Larry Geller said, "their relationship never seemed to progress beyond an eighth-grade date." Priscilla was expected to look pretty, smile, never have problems, fix his dinner exactly as he liked, and be prepared to go along with his double standard. In her book, **Elvis and Me,** Priscilla describes Elvis as being "her father, God and lover." He taught her everything—how to dress, apply make-up, what to think, and how to behave. Starting at fourteen!

His girlfriends, after his divorce from Priscilla, described being with Elvis this way: The first night you're his hot high school date, then you graduate to being his mother—getting him endless bottled waters, feeding him Jello, listening to him read spiritual texts, and talking baby talk. The one woman who shared his spiritual search and was not a glamorous sex kitten was his back-up singer, Kathy Westmoreland. When she insisted that adultery didn't jibe with spirituality, Elvis became furious, shouting that he didn't believe in marriage. He fumed, "What am I supposed to do, train up some other woman so she knows how to behave around me?"

Elvis the sexist. That hurts. Equally disappointing was the squandering of his talent in inane movies and tacky career moves—not from Elvis's own self-indulgence or laziness (those came later), but because he couldn't stand up and talk back to male authority figures. These included all his movie directors, as well as his manager, who someone described as "a tasteless carny barker with a power over Elvis he used ruthlessly." The one time Elvis did talk back, the result was the "Comeback Special." The Colonel imagined a schmaltzy Christmas show with a bubble machine, happy kiddies, and Elvis in a dark suit and tie. Instead, Elvis did Elvis—in black leather belting out rockers and crooning ballads; in a red suit and scarf shouting gospel; and in a luminous white one crying out "If I Can Dream."

But the thing that really hurts is my discovery that his spiritual search was as sexist as his love life. He told Priscilla when he started meditating that he needed to be celibate. In his last serious relationship with Ginger Alden, he informed Larry Geller that it was more spiritual than any of his others, because he had no carnal desire. To his credit, Larry didn't think this reflected any newfound holiness, but rather Elvis's need to cover up his impotence.

So much for the reconciliation of Saturday night and Sunday morning. No matter how much I want him to be whole, Elvis remained split. One Elvis was a devoted son, husband, and father, while another whored around in Las Vegas, staying up all night and sleeping all day, explaining, "I reckon folks like to be out at night because God can't see." One Elvis gave away two billion dollars and another raced around like a perpetual adolescent joyriding on motorcycles, playing increasingly brutal contact sports, and collecting guns and police badges. One Elvis read spiritual books, meditated, and endlessly toured "to spread Jesus' message of love," while another ate and drugged himself to death on fried banana and peanut butter sandwiches and twenty kinds of prescription painkillers.

I wander around shell-shocked, alternating between wanting to throw up and wanting to cry. Claudia finds my behavior excessive; she can't understand how real my relationship with Elvis feels. I read her a chapter from Erika Doss's *Elvis Culture*, describing interviews with dozens of women who have had an intimate, often lifelong relationship with a dead Elvis. Many have created huge altars from Elvis memorabilia. All believe he has helped them to have better lives, including going to college, ending abusive relationships, or finding God.

I want Elvis's life to be golden, filled with music and purpose and joy. I want him to live happily ever after. I want him to reconcile the opposites his music did. I want this so much it keeps me up at night with stomach cramps. For my own health, I have to get Elvis out of my life. I swear off listening to him sing for a few days, then go back, unable to resist. But I only go back to playing the gospel. Even though I love his rock 'n' roll, it makes me uneasy. As if something in it is the source of everything that went wrong, not just for him, but for all of us.

I decide that what went wrong isn't the ecstasy or the body; it's the sexual excess, materialism, and no-limits which rock culture spawned. If you suddenly lift centuries of repression, then sex, feelings, and fun can get ugly—and for Elvis they did, as if his amazing freedom train turned around and ran right over his life with Elvis asleep at the wheel. Lester Bangs, *The Village Voice* music critic, wrote after Elvis died:

> Literally, anytime this man moved the slightest part of his body tens of thousand of people went berserk....The rest of us are still reeling from the impact. Sexual chaos reigns currently, but out of that chaos may flow true understanding and harmony, and either way, Elvis almost single-handedly opened the floodgates.

The next time Allyn calls from his cottage, I read him that last line. "What do you think?"

"Well, he's right about the sexual chaos. But I think cultures are like individuals. Symptoms represent our inadequate, but necessary, attempts to heal ourselves. Sometimes a culture has to break down to break through. I've watched my clients and the culture as a whole struggle with sexual issues since the fifties—first with repression, then with freedom and all the problems of promiscuity, unwed mothers and divorce that followed."

"But why should that be? Sexual energy for me is about renewal and connection, pleasure, joy..."

"Not as long as sex is mixed up with all our personal and cultural baggage. Anyway, how's life with Elvis?"

"Not that great," I sigh. "His music makes me so happy and his life makes me sick."

When I hang up, it occurs to me that whatever kind of song he's singing, Elvis takes me into my body in a joyous way. How can you love any other body if you don't love and enjoy your own? If you fear your body—its insistent desires, its inconvenient feelings, its vulnerability and inevitable death—won't you fear other bodies and try to control or blame them. Hasn't that been the way of things since Adam blamed Eve and Eve blamed the snake?

I'd had the same questions last summer when our book group read **Reading Lolita in Tehran.** It was eerie to see the same dismissal of joy and the body in the horrors that beset Mullah-ruled Iran: the female body literally blacked out in chadors, the banning of music, dance, poetry, and any public expressions of humor, happiness, or affection; the glorification of martyrdom and death—fountains spilling red water like blood, and ten-year-olds, wearing little keys to heaven, sent off to battle Iraqis; the brutal torture and execution of the tens of thousands brave enough to protest. And all of this so that the God-fearing citizens of Iran might finally get to a paradise where the physical pleasures banned on earth await them.

    Maybe that's why I hear Elvis say, I swear it, "Stay with me, baby, this has a happy ending." In the meantime, my heart hurts. Sometimes I wish I'd never read all the books that revealed every Elvis flaw. I want my Saturday-night-Sunday-morning back.

Compassion is the highest form of intelligence.

George Bernard Shaw

9.
Love Him Tender

It is the first day of August. I think maybe I need to give up my Elvis mania. It's taking up way too much time, not to mention money. The fact is I'm getting a little fed up with Elvis. Now, when I look at my photograph books, I can see all the tawdry tinsel-town materialism of Elvis's poverty mentality and, despite Gladys's noblest efforts, the limitations of his dirt-poor upbringing. I can see how his vibrant sexuality, genuine sweetness, and authentic nonconformity gradually changed over time—as if a butterfly had turned into a caterpillar.

The one high note, soaring all the way through, was the voice and the talent. Even in the pre-filming for his last television special, where he looked like an ill-made souvenir of himself, he sang "Unchained Melody" with feeling and delicacy. He sang it solo, accompanying himself on the piano. In two months he would be dead.

So the question I have to ask myself on this August day is, "Can I really stick around with this guy who has made such a mess of his life, or do I need to cut and run?" That night I have this dream:

> *I live in a tiny tar paper shack and give birth to a baby boy with a shock of jet-black hair. He can walk and talk immediately. He takes my hand and leads me to the back door. The creaky unpainted wood barely hangs on its hinges. It opens into a beautiful garden. In the center are seven ascending pools carved out of a small mountain. The baby climbs up to each pool. At each level, he becomes slightly larger. When he reaches the top, he turns. It's Elvis, of course, resplendent in his white "If I Can Dream" suit. He's reaching his hand out to me.*

I wake up muttering impatiently, "Oh, for heaven's sakes." I guess I have more to learn from Elvis.

I decide the place to start is with this whole business of loving. Clearly, whatever I think I'm doing with Elvis is imaginary. And yet it isn't. I know more about him and have spent more quality time with him than I have with a lot of other men I've known. That's what I need to get back to. Can I love Elvis through sickness and health, good times and bad? But that's not the way of romance. Romance so easily becomes contempt, unless you make the leap into compassion.

There's a passage in *To Kill A Mockingbird* where Scout says, "If you want to understand someone you have to get inside his skin and really wriggle around in it."

I use my next morning walks just this way—to pretend I'm Elvis and try to feel my way into the tragedy of his life. I remind myself to tread carefully here. I don't want to bury Elvis's extraordinary talent and charisma under a barrage of psychobabble, or demean his spirituality and originality with cheap excuses. But there are so many.

From the time success knocked at his door right up until he died, Elvis, who was too fearful to sleep in the dark or alone, had a recurring nightmare: all his money was gone, the fans had abandoned him, and the Colonel had left. Shame intensified Elvis's terror of poverty and abandonment. Despite Gladys's attempts to keep some soul and dignity in the family with her impeccable housekeeping, religious beliefs, and insistence on good manners, the Presleys had never been more than one step away from being white trash. Elvis grew up without running water, electricity, or a toilet. Food was a luxury. The first thing Elvis did with his wealth was to gorge on food, eating as many as twenty burgers at a time. Sun Records producer Sam Phillips observed, "Unlike middle-class sixties hippies, Elvis was a nonconformist, not a rebel. He wanted in, not out."

Throughout his childhood and adolescence, his peers bullied him ceaselessly. In elementary school, Elvis was a target because his father had been in Parchman prison. In middle school, he was picked on because he looked poor and weird with his long hair and workman's overalls. In high school, the shout, "Look at that squirrel just come down from his tree," became the signal to beat up Elvis. Sam Phillips, who first recorded him, said, "Elvis Presley was probably innately the most introverted person that ever came into my studio. He tried not to show it, but he felt so inferior. His insecurity was so markedly like that of a black person." Yet Elvis, rather than being bitter, seemed determined to win everyone over. In his last year in high school, he won the talent contest and all his peers cheered. He ran back to the teacher who had pushed him to compete, sobbing and laughing, "They like me, they really like me." Steve Binder, Elvis's producer for the Comeback Special, said that Elvis drove him crazy, perpetually asking, "What if they don't like me?"

Despite his fame, Elvis felt unloved and alone. He lamented to country singer T. J. Sheppard in Vegas, "Those people don't love me in a personal way, they don't know what's inside me." To Larry Geller he said, "Nobody seems to understand that I'm a human being too: I'll never know if a woman loves me or Elvis Presley." His cousin Alan Greenwood writes that Elvis grew furious, and then depressed, when he realized most women were disappointed in his lovemaking. They expected ELVIS.

The early death of Gladys, the one person he could be sure loved and believed in him, compounded his sense of isolation. Even Priscilla couldn't understand the spiritual concerns central to him. She set two conditions for their marriage—get rid of Larry and burn all the spiritual books. Elvis had no male mentors who genuinely cared about him as a spiritual person and an artist. His father never stopped being an adolescent practical joker and lay-about. The Colonel exploited him. The Memphis Mafia were basically good old boys whose interests gravitated to sex, fast cars, and partying. Larry was Elvis's age and more of a brother than a guide. He had no real authority to confront the *King*.

The question I can't let go of is: "Why wasn't Elvis able to use his spiritual practices to make his life work?" Finally, in desperation, I call Harvey. We talk about Elvis for a whole afternoon in Claudia's gazebo. Harvey wonders why I haven't thought more about the corrosive effects of his early and all-pervasive fame. How could anyone really pursue a spiritual path when everyone around him thought and acted like he was God? It would have required far more inner awareness than one could expect of any twenty-year-old. And unlike a Bob Dylan or John Lennon, Elvis was a pleaser; he needed people to love him. He short-circuited his own development as a person and an artist by becoming what his fans and the Colonel wanted.

"Everything you're telling me says Elvis was a genuine spiritual seeker," Harvey says. "I didn't know about that side of Elvis. My father was a Missouri Synod Lutheran minister who thought Elvis was taking every teenager straight to hell."

He tells me he thinks that Elvis's spiritual search degenerated into an escape from dealing directly with all his underlying psychological issues. Elvis read about spiritual ideas and meditated, rather than asking himself why he couldn't sleep at night, what was he so afraid of, why was he making crappy movies, and why was he cheating on his wife if he loved her. "For Elvis to find inner peace, he would have had to confront his demons," Harvey says. "He didn't have a mentor or a circle of friends to help him."

"I think it's worse than that. Elvis was so completely alone. No one loved him. Everyone was using him or awed by him."

It just makes me so sad for Elvis. I feel my eyes welling up. For some reason I'm thinking about Maureen Stapleton's description of meeting Elvis at a screen test. She was terrified and had her son Danny with her. Elvis had finished his test, but noticed how scared she looked. He told her he felt the same way most of the time and that she would do fine. He even offered to watch her son. After the test, she came out and saw Danny totally absorbed in some guitar chords Elvis was showing him. Elvis saw her, asked how it went, then said, "Goodbye, ma'am." He opened the door to a crowd of screaming fans. Stapleton suddenly realized how amazing his empathy and his lack of pretense and self-absorption were. There are so many Elvis stories like that. How did it all go so wrong?

"You know," Harvey says, putting his arm around my shoulder, "what I really think is that Elvis presented an ecstatic possibility that fifties America repressed. He couldn't bring Saturday night and Sunday morning together in his own life because the culture couldn't."

"And huge parts of it still can't! Now we're waist-deep in explicit sex and sexual messages that are totally disconnected from our souls. It's like we all took the Saturday night side of Elvis and forgot the Sunday morning."

"And in reaction," Harvey adds, "the Christian fundamentalists are back. If you think about it, the eastern spirituality Elvis encountered is just as stuck in the mind/body split. Sex and enjoyment aren't up there with prayer and service. In fact, women and the body are usually viewed as hindrances to a spiritual life. Elvis didn't stand a chance."

That evening I find myself wishing that instead of sharing Elvis with Allyn, I could share Allyn with Elvis. When Allyn calls that night, I tell him about my afternoon with Harvey and ask, "What would you have done if you'd had the chance to work with Elvis?"

"Well, in a funny way I came close. In the early sixties I worked with a young woman, a devout Christian Scientist, who claimed to have had a relationship with Elvis. Naturally, I thought she was fantasizing, but she brought in a photo album of their time together in Los Angeles when he was recording for RCA. She said Elvis was as serious about spirituality as she was, but she broke it off because she felt his desire for the fast life became greater than his desire for God."

"Did you think that?" I ask. (Allyn's story amazes me. How does he manage to touch the hem of practically everyone's garment?)

"It seemed to me he was driven by his immense ambition to be somebody for himself and Gladys and his enormous talent. He wasn't self-aware enough to carry so much charisma and charge. It's like an electric wire. If you run too much power through it, it blows up. Elvis got too famous, too fast."

Then he deflects my question back to me, "What do you think?" I tell him that everything he's said about Elvis makes sense, but I can't help feeling Elvis's self-destructiveness had something to do with Gladys. I think he blamed himself for her early death. After he made his first million, she wanted him to quit, settle down and buy a furniture store. She was the most important person in his life and his moral compass. He knew she would have totally disapproved of his divorce and his lifestyle.

When we finally hang up, I feel sad for Elvis all over again.

****

I go by myself to Quaker meeting on a Sunday early in August. I'm sweltering and sticky and wondering about Elvis: Who knows what combination of genes, character, circumstances, and luck grace or disgrace a life? A woman stands up to speak. She ends with a quote she attributes to Gandhi, "If we could read the secret story of those we hate, we would find in each person's life, sorrow and suffering enough to disarm all our anger." And all our disappointment, too.

I'm on one of my morning walks when I hear this loud voice in my head. It's that strident know-it-all James Carville, Bill Clinton's campaign manager. He's shouting, "It's the music, stupid!"

"No!" I want to yell back. "It's the compassion, stupid!" I don't want to discount what opening my heart to Elvis has done for me. Compassion feels as joyful as ecstasy and delight. It's more subdued and tender, but I have the same sensation of being less a separate self and more a part of everyone else.

I have tried the Buddhist practice of *lovingkindness* meditation for years. With it, you ask that all beings be happy and free, starting with people you love, then people you feel neutral about, and then people you hate. The practice definitely moves me in a kinder direction. But maybe I'm missing some Buddhist brain wiring because it still feels like a *practice*—as if I'm rehearsing something, rather than playing full out from my heart. But my experience with Elvis—of figuratively wriggling around in his skin—is so compelling; I decide to try my Elvis-compassion-practice on my father.

Our relationship has always been strained. After my mother left him, I didn't see him until my freshman year in college. The visit was a disaster. Between his critical eye and scathing tongue, I gained fifty pounds in three months and had a mini-nervous breakdown. We have made sporadic contact over the years, but I decided that for my own mental health it was best not to see too much of him.

On my next few morning walks, I try to see his life through his eyes, rather than through my own glass darkly. What must it have been like for him to be a boy genius who knew by age four he wanted to be an architect? His mother, a Jewish immigrant with her own sad history, believed his brilliance would justify her life. He went to Harvard at sixteen and became the golden-haired boy of Walter Gropius, the famous Bauhaus architect. He won a number of important architectural contests. Then things soured: his style didn't fit with postmodernism and he never created a building up to his own standards. Several wives left him.

I realize that feeling compassion for my father will be harder than for Elvis; Elvis only wounded my illusions. Still, witnessing my father's life from within, and with a little distance from my own, begins to change something in me. I decide to write him. Maybe I'll even go see him in the fall.

But Carville is right. It *is* the music. No one is still trying to understand Beethoven's nastiness or worrying about Mozart's philandering, practical jokes, and obsession with becoming an honorary member of the Vienna police force. So what was it that made Elvis an international icon in life and death? Why *did* Leonard Bernstein call him the most important cultural phenomenon of the 20th century? How did Elvis bring the beat to everything, and why does it matter?

The only question to ask of any work of art is:

How deep is the life from which it springs?

James Joyce

10.
The Love That's Wantin' t' Come into The World

It's the middle of August. The air is no longer southern sultry; it has a hint of the sharp dry edge that augurs a Wisconsin summer's end. I'm starting to think my Elvis thing is a lot bigger than I am. There might be something to my Quaker vision after all. Maybe Elvis really is the cultural hero I'd imagined him to be back in June.

Our August book group meeting is at Harvey's. We sit comfortably on his sprawling, veranda-like front porch. Night comes earlier. It will be our last time with Jean Houston's book, **The Hero and the Goddess**. The fireflies are batting their lights at one another in one last fling before fall. We're still waiting for Odessa to arrive. While everyone else is getting brownies and coffee, Harvey asks me if I saw the History Channel special, "Ten Days That Changed America." It included an hour each on Lincoln's assassination, the murder of the three civil rights workers in Mississippi, the first test of the atomic bomb, and Elvis's 1956 appearance on the Ed Sullivan show.

Harvey wonders if the Elvis episode is a ploy, just a way to sell the accompanying DVD. He could be right. According to *Business Weekly,* Elvis's name is gold. You are more likely to sell anything with his name, rather than anyone else's, attached to it. But I remind Harvey of the line under my Krishna montage: "Elvis brought us a dance it took a whole civilization to forget and ten seconds into the Ed Sullivan show to remember."

"So what do you think that means?" I ask him.

"It means that Elvis turned two thousand years of Christian body-hatred upside down and sent two hundred and fifty years of American Puritanism right down the drain. It means life is not just a dreary vale of tears and unremitting work and grimness but the place where heaven is found."

I'm impressed. I've never heard Harvey sound so passionate. Still, I want him to go deeper, but neither of us has the words quite yet. It's something about how dance connects us to a great mystery that poets and prophets have always intuited: that the body is holy, that sex is holy, that rhythm and dance bring you closer to spirit. And there's something about the mystery of feeling—how all feeling is of the body, and how, without feeling, religion is just dry commandments bereft of love. Elvis unleashed this mystery for an entire culture. Michael Ventura writes, "His moves were body shouts and our bodies heard him. No one has ever seen a white boy move like that."

Odessa arrives and we start with the question we always ask on our last time together with a book: "What about this book engages your own life?" When it's my turn to answer, I read the sentence from Jean Houston's introduction that I've underlined three times in the last three months—words that have given me so much comfort whenever I've had serious doubts about myself and Elvis: "Mythical archetypes can become spiritual partners with whom we engage in soul-making."

That night I have another Elvis dream:

In the middle of a bucolic field is a small cathedral. Next to it is a convent. I knock on the convent door. It's opened by a beautiful woman—long flowing hair, luscious lips and a soft sensuous habit. "You're just in time for the Rave Mass," she says, leading me quickly into the cathedral sanctuary. There are hundreds of people. I can't figure how such a small cathedral holds so many. The priest ascends to the altar. It's Bono, the rock star who's trying to end world poverty and AIDS. He's surrounded by a lot of techno stuff. He starts pushing buttons and the cathedral is flooded with colored lights and the pounding heartbeat of millennium pop. Images flash all over the wall—pictures of Martin Luther King, Gandhi, Einstein, Bill Gates, Shakespeare, the Himalayas, whales, raindrops on a rose—hundreds of them. Elvis in full regalia flashes before us. "Elvis was a prophet!" Bono shouts. Everyone is whirling like Dervishes. Then it all stops. Bono invites us to exchange the kiss of peace. People kiss me passionately on the lips. "Don't forget the lambs; don't forget the sheep!" Bono calls out to us. For a second, I wonder if the sanctuary is going to fill up with farm animals. Then I remember the New Testament.

I wake up exhilarated. I'm so glad I took a chance on Elvis. My dream is so spangly, gaudy and over the top, it's like an e-mail from him from some heavenly Las Vegas: Willow,/ Love your body. Love spirit. Love your neighbor. Take good care of every body./ Elvis.

Then I feel miserable. More than anything I wish Elvis were alive, not in my head, but really alive, sitting beside me. I want to tell him that it doesn't matter about all that mess in the end. I want to tell him that he's loved, he's missed, he's a cultural hero. Shortly before Elvis's death, Joe Esposito (one of the few friends who stood by him to the end) said that Elvis was actually afraid no one would remember him or his music after he died.

****

It is the Labor Day holiday, the last official weekend of summer in Wisconsin. Saturday night I go to the Rhythm and Blues Fest at Warner Park with Harvey and his wife, Jean. The Reverend Al Green is headlining the show. The Reverend comes on stage. He is old, his frizzy hair shot through with gray, but his unlined cocoa-brown skin shines. He winks at us and says (as best as I can remember), "You know, I started out in the church a long time ago. I left to play the devil's music because I wanted to rock 'n' roll, but I had a lot of trouble with women and some near calls with the law, and I went back to the church. But now I'm singing rhythm and blues and gospel because, guess what, brothers and sisters, it's all the same kind of love." Then he opens his mouth really wide and out comes "Take Me to the River," just about the "churchiest" street shout imaginable.

Only one person does Saturday night and Sunday morning better. That night I go home and dance with him. And I make a promise to myself: Sometime soon, Elvis and I are going to teach Allyn to dance.

Everything in the universe has a rhythm. Everything dances.

Maya Angelou

Epilogue

Claudia and I are having late morning coffee in her gazebo. It's sunny, but the air is fresh and crisp like eating a tart autumn apple. The leaves are beginning to change color and we're expecting the cedar waxwings who always stop by her backyard in the fall. Our schedules are so out of sync, I've actually made an appointment to see her. I want her to tell me how to teach someone to dance. She looks at me cagily. "You mean teach Allyn to dance, right?" She's skeptical; she's known Allyn a lot longer than I have.

"I wouldn't even bother trying to teach that old dog any new tricks," she says with a snort. She finds my Elvis "promise" hilarious. "Besides, you'll always be battling the ghosts of Mrs. Gustafson's School of the Dance and Ethel Lamott."

"Who's she?"

"He's never told you about Ethel Lamott?"

Apparently Allyn had described her to Claudia as just about the least attractive girl he'd ever seen—and the tallest. He had to steer her around the dance floor in

P.E. for twelve years, because the teachers lined them up by heights to dance.

"Well, just forget it's Allyn." I know Claudia has taught lots of guys to dance, including her newest boyfriend. "How do you do it?"

"First, you've got to get them to feel the rhythm. People who can't dance live from the neck up. All that mental stuff keeps them from feeling the beat in their bodies and surrendering to it."

"And you do that by…"

Now Claudia is totally engaged. She loves to teach. "I have them get behind me and put their hands on my hips. I move to the beat and they feel the rhythm. Then I turn and let them lead. When they lose the beat, I have them put their hands on my hips again."

My late morning coffee with Claudia has made my usual morning walk an afternoon one. Maybe she's right and I'm on the wrong track trying to get Allyn to dance. I'm not so sure Allyn can't feel the beat; he's just not interested. On the other hand, *dance* is just a codeword for bringing more Saturday night into our relationship, which is a little skewed towards Sunday morning.

I'll have to approach Allyn delicately. A full frontal assault won't work; he responds to subtlety. On one of our first "Saturday nights," I dressed up in a delicate white corselet and white stockings with a circle of real roses in my hair. I instinctively knew black would be a total turn-off. When I emerged from the bathroom, Allyn feigned alarm as if aliens had landed.

"What *are* you doing in that get-up?" he asked.

****

It's late September and I'm not making much progress on my promise. I wish Elvis would help me, but he seems to have temporarily left my building. I haven't dreamt of him in weeks.

Allyn and I are at the Edgewater Hotel. He asks me if I feel comfortable leaving my clients for ten days and going with him to Marquette. He always goes back the last week in September to close up camp. I say yes, even though it will be more work than pleasure. The fall colors are awfully alluring. The cold nights make the leaves in the Upper Peninsula like no others. Every leaf looks lit from within, as if the sun they are made of is shining forth.

I take my CD player and some Elvis tapes along. I still haven't given up the idea of dancing. Allyn wants to hear more about my summer with Elvis, and it occurs to me he might want to hear some of his music. We haven't had time to talk about Elvis in depth, and the six-hour drive to the Upper Peninsula provides the perfect opportunity. Allyn will have lots of questions and he will listen as if our conversation is all that exist. I asked him where he learned to do that—it's such a rare quality, even in a psychotherapist. He made light of it, saying, "I wish it came from a spiritual place, but it has a lot more to do with how shy I was as an adolescent. Asking questions and listening was one way I trained myself not to be shy."

Allyn wants to know how I'm a different person having spent a summer with Elvis.

"There's just so much, I don't know where to start."

"So do what you tell your clients to do. 'Take a breath and say whatever comes up.'"

Elvis, I tell him, brought me back to my senses, literally. Singing and dancing, touching and tasting, hearing and seeing became my meditation practice. And ecstasy, more than mindfulness or silence, took me out of myself. It was as if everything invited me to dance and to fall in love. Whether my partner was another person, a tree, or a cup of tea, we were both held by something larger than ourselves.

Allyn listens so raptly, my words seem to take flight. "I know it sounds counter-intuitive," I continue, "but pleasure didn't make me more self-absorbed." I tell him I've never felt so happy or so spiritually alive. Even in July when the ecstasy went sour, it turned into compassion. And compassion felt like another form of joy—expansive and tender. I stepped outside my opinionated little self and loved Elvis as he was, not as I wanted him to be.

I wonder if Allyn thinks I'm exaggerating, but he says, "I guess spiritual teachers come in all sizes."

"You think that about Elvis?"

"Absolutely. Elvis gave you a real gift. But I wonder why he couldn't give it to himself?"

"But he did, at least in the beginning." He was just as surprised, I tell Allyn, by the power of ecstasy in himself as he was by its effect on everyone else. His biographer Peter Guralnick said that Elvis never did understand his angry critics or his sexual magnetism.

"I don't know what happened to Elvis," I say. "Sometimes I think he was a little bit like Moses: he had a vision of the Promised Land, he could point the way. He just never got there."

I also tell Allyn that I didn't just learn about ecstasy and a new way of everyday spirituality from Elvis, I also learned things about myself—places where I'm stuck, and where our relationship might be.

Allyn says he's really interested in that, but he wants to be fresh for it. "We've got ten more days. Let's give Elvis a rest, okay?"

"Okay," I agree, and find myself actually feeling a little relieved. Talking about Elvis is easy. I'm not so sure talking about us will be. Allyn turns on the radio to get the news. We drive along in companionable silence as the landscape changes from tidy farms and small towns to the wild Northwoods.

It's already dusk by the time we get to Marquette. Allyn's camp is about twenty minutes outside of town right on the edge of Lake Superior, nestled among immense boulders that are the remains of a mountain chain older than the Himalayas. We drive up a long narrow road with towering red and white pines on either side. When we park, we still have a quarter-mile hike up a steep path past small jack pine, low bush blueberries, and over jagged, moss-covered rocks. At the top, the infinite expanse of Lake Superior looms.

A jerrybuilt combination of pine logs and stone steps winds among the lichen-covered boulders down a steep vertical incline to Allyn's camp. His cabin looks like a Japanese teahouse sprung from the rocks full grown. The tar paper covering it—gray-green and spotted with lichen—mimics the rocks perfectly.

We go in, past the glassed-in porch, through the living room and its hand-hewn stone fireplace, and put all our provisions in the tiny kitchen galley. Unmatched china and a variety of glasses line the shelves, along with the covered tins that are Allyn's main weapon in his perpetual battle with mice. I put my suitcase on one of the bunk beds in the narrow backroom and head to the outhouse in back.

It's only eight o'clock, but between the long drive and hiking up the hill carrying twenty pounds of stuff, I'm exhausted. I hug Allyn good-night and fall into my bunk. A few hours later, I wake up shivering. It's so cold I can blow steam out of my mouth. Yoopers—people who live in the Upper Peninsula year-round—like to say there are only three seasons in the UP: July, August, and winter.

In the morning we go into town for breakfast at the Verling, a popular watering hole and eatery since 1865. All the Yoopers that Allyn has known from childhood hang out here. From our table I can see the lake and Thill's fish house where we'll buy whitefish, caught just this morning, for dinner. Allyn wants to continue our Elvis conversation.

"So, what does your summer with Elvis mean for us?" he asks.

"Oh, probably that we should do a lot more dancing," I say flippantly. I don't want to get into a deep conversation with him here. It's so noisy and some friend of his is sure to interrupt.

Happily, we're interrupted by Dan and Kathleen. Dan is the son of one of Allyn's oldest Yooper friends, Fred. Dan is big and burly like his dad, but quieter and more intellectual. For the last five years, he's seriously considered a religious vocation. I'm glad he's chosen to be with Kathleen and to work as a spiritual counselor instead. Kathleen's a tall, raw-boned farm girl and a poet. She just came back from Antarctica, where a team of scientists commissioned her to write about their work.

"Tell us about Elvis," Kathleen shouts out in her usual state of excitement. Allyn apparently regaled them all summer with tales of "Graceland in Wisconsin." We tell them we've got errands to do now, but suggest dinner next Saturday.

Three hours and six stores later, we're on our way back to camp. From the car I can see Marquette's Protestant cemetery—a grand affair filled with marble mausoleums that mark the passing of the robber barons and village elders who made their fortunes up here in iron ore and lumber. In the cemetery, a stand of sugar maples blazes like a living Rose Window of Chartres, their crimson leaves and black branches backlit by the sun. I ask Allyn if we have time to stop. I *want* those leaves.

While I frenetically fill a plastic bag, Allyn wanders among the graves. He is completely absorbed in Marquette history and every grave prompts a memory. "Hey!" he shouts. "You'll never guess whose grave I've found!" It's Mrs. Gustafson's. Allyn's bouncing up and down on it. "Do you know how long I've waited to do this?"

"Wait a second, you might as well do it right. I'll go get Elvis." I run back to the car and get the CD player. Out blasts "If I Can Dream." I put Allyn's hands on my hips and shake away. Allyn grins. He's definitely dancing, but hardly ecstatic.

"Made my day," he gasps when he stops a few minutes later, a little short of breath. Then he looks down. "And probably poor old Mrs. Gustafson's. I can still hear her, 'Now, come on, Allyn, let's see a smile.'"

Back in the car, I ask Allyn if he knows what Herman Hesse, one of his and Elvis's favorite authors, said about dance. I read from a quote I've pasted on the back of my CD player. "So you can't dance? Not at all? Not one step? How can you say you've taken the trouble to live, when you can't even dance?"

Allyn pretends to scowl. "That doesn't sound like Hesse at all," he says, "unless he's using 'dance' as code for something else. Did you know that I stopped by Hesse's house when I was in Europe in the sixties? I really wanted to meet him. I heard he'd taken a year off to meditate before he could complete the last chapter of **Siddhartha,** and I wanted to know more about that. When I got there, there was a sign on the gate: 'I am an old man and I need quiet. Please go away.'"

We spend the afternoon putting up the winter shutters. Each of them is about five feet long and difficult to maneuver. I'm grateful we won't have to struggle with the forty-foot pipes that extend from the house into the lake until the day we leave. Later, Allyn broils the whitefish and fries up potatoes with the oyster mushrooms we found on our evening walk in the woods. We eat on the porch that's still warm from the day's sun.

Allyn holds a piece of whitefish up on his fork and waves it around, saying, "You learn something about the distilled essence of Lake Superior, literally at a gut level, if you eat what comes from it."

"That it's especially good with olive oil and lemon?" I tease, taking my third helping. I've forgotten how hungry hard work and long walks make me. And exhausted. Once again, I flop into my bunk at eight, leaving Allyn reading by the fire he built after dinner.

That night I have my first Elvis dream in almost a month:

I'm in Maui at one of those white-stucco honeymoon hotels that look like monumental Taj Mahals dedicated to love. Lotus-filled ponds nestle among perfumed gardens teeming with butterflies. I walk down a long hallway that goes from the gift shop to a soft, white-sand pathway leading down to the ocean. The hallway is lined with airbrushed paintings in delicate sunrise pinks and ocean blues. I look at them closely and am surprised to see a nude couple in many poses—swimming among dolphins and spiral waves, making love inside the unfurling petals of a giant rose, dancing with cranes, cradled within a huge seashell.

A white sign describes the paintings as "Postcards From a Romance." Even though they are many times the size of a postcard, the sign makes dream sense. They seem to be sent from another dimension where all the sometimes warring opposites of this one—self and other, male and female, nature and spirit—are reconciled.

I continue walking towards the ocean past the striped tents where honeymooning couples meet for moonlight assignations. On the beach I watch the sunset melt into the sea. Then I smell an intense musky scent, like Jovan, Elvis's favorite aftershave. I turn and see Elvis walking toward me wearing slacks and a Hawaiian shirt, draped with a lei. He sits down beside me, and I immediately start jabbering about the paintings.

Elvis puts his index finger to his lips. "I really like those paintings, too," he says. "Reconciling opposites. Yeah, man, that's what LOVE does. Love's all I was singing about. Sometimes I wonder if anybody got it."

I want to say, "I did," but I feel shy. I ask him about Allyn instead. He takes my hand. His hand is so much smoother and softer than mine. The caramel-colored skin glows.

"Honey," he says, "There's a whole lotta ways t' dance."

My eyes open abruptly. I'm back in the cold and suddenly aware that Elvis doesn't feel like my lover anymore, at least not in my dreams. He's more like a wonderful older brother. And those dream pictures—I want to paint them! It hadn't occurred to me before that there are endless images of naked women in Western painting and almost none of naked couples. Certainly there are none of lovers dancing with a world that's dancing back.

After breakfast, Allyn suggests we walk on the birch trail to what we've named "The Red Pine Cathedral." One-hundred-foot-high Norway pines tower in a half-circle like the ribs of a gothic cathedral, or a great choir. Long rays of morning light stream down through the pines, making a circle of white light on the ground where we stand. "Those pines are almost one hundred and fifty years old," Allyn says. "They were saplings when Harlow Clark set up the first camp in Marquette not five miles from here."

Allyn notices that I'm not really listening. I'm standing on one foot slowly waving my arms and moving my hands like a Balinese temple dancer.

"What are you doing?" he asks. "Yoga?"

"Nope, I'm dancing." I tell him I got the idea from a dream I had last night, and I describe the paintings where couples are moving with the energies of flowers and birds and the ocean. "It's like everything has a rhythm and you can dance with it."

Allyn closes his eyes and stands on one leg. He's so tall and still, he looks more like one of the pines than I do. I wonder if you can dance without moving. Then I realize we're both doing what Nellie taught me to do years ago. Navajos attune to the energies of mountains, water, and plants. When Navajos hunt deer, they try to walk and breathe like a deer, to cherish the deer and then become a deer. "You can find the deer in the trees," say the old ones, "if you have the deer in the heart."

When we get back to camp, Allyn makes coffee and toasts up some of his friend Bob's "pretty good bread," as Bob calls it. We take everything out to the porch. I spread the toast with the thimbleberry jam Allyn made this summer. He wants to know more about my dream, which I describe in detail.

"You need to paint what you saw," he says. I nod in agreement. Then Allyn asks the question I realize I've been avoiding.

"Something about the way you talk and dream about Elvis makes me think you might be dissatisfied with us. True?"

I want to be straight with Allyn, but I find myself edging sidewise into his question and choosing my words very carefully. "First you need to know," I begin, "that if nothing in our relationship changes, that's fine with me. I know you have a very different way of accessing and expressing spirit than I do, but it's your top priority. I'm easily distracted and you keep me on the straight and narrow. That is very, very important to me."

"And you do the same for me," he says.

"I do?"

"Of course, why do you think I've been hanging out with you for fifteen years?"

I sit back for a moment pondering Allyn's question. In response, I tell him the story of the Tibetan monk and his Bengali tea-boy. The Bengali tea-boy is a bad-tempered, spiritual neophyte, but for the monk, he's like the irritant that grows the pearl. I'm teasing, but a part of me has felt this way from our first encounter, so the question I ask is genuine. "How do I do that for you?"

"Partly through the intensity of your seeking and the strange paths it takes you on. I'm not someone who's going to go gaga about Elvis or poetry or a flower, but when I borrow your eyes, I see that this world is a very, very good place to be." He laughs. "You're my spiritual finishing school."

"Well, why haven't you ever told me?" I'm surprised how hungry I am for those words and how afraid I've been to ask for them, as if that hunger might somehow be unspiritual.

"'Cause I'm a shy guy, for heaven's sake. Don't you remember that early in our relationship you suspected I was an introvert? I score one-hundred percent on tests for introversion."

It's true. Even though Allyn seemed so out in the world, there was something not quite spontaneous about his social interactions, like someone who's just learning how to dance and trying to remember the steps. When I asked him about it, he said, "I trained myself not be shy."

"Wait a minute," I say, wanting to get back to me, and to something else I realize I'm hungry for. "So why have you never told me you love me?" I remind him that when we made love early on he talked about 'no special relationship,' except with the Mystery."

"I think I was testing you and you passed the test."

"But you still never say you love *me*."

"It's not about saying, it's about the way I am with you. That word has become so sentimentalized, it almost has no meaning. Besides, you never asked."

"Well, as long as I'm your spiritual finishing school," I begin teasingly, "this is what needs to happen: more wildness, more fun, more dancing—a whole curriculum of ecstasy."

Allyn takes my hand and holds it quietly. Finally he asks, "What do you really want me to do?"

"Maybe that's something for you to meditate on," I say gently.

****

We spend the day before we leave winterizing the cabin. Allyn's been closing camp for forty years and everything has to be done just so. It occurs to me this would be a lot more fun to the tune of Elvis, but I decide not to push Allyn when his "old maid" is in high gear. Together we shutter the porch windows, drain all the indoor pipes, and put anti-freeze in them. The fireplace has to be covered by a screen and the chimney plugged up. Allyn tells me dire stories of people who don't do this—squirrels come down covered with soot and race around wreaking havoc. While Allyn checks out how hard it will be to remove the pipes tomorrow, I pour a quart of hot lime down the outhouse hole.

In the late afternoon, we drive into town to meet Dan and Kathleen at Vango's for Greek pizza. Dan immediately asks me about Elvis. He wonders if I'm being serious or ironic.

"Absolutely serious," I say. I tell him about Saturday night and Sunday morning, and add, "My journey with Elvis has a lot in common with your own."

"It does?"

"Sure, reconciling your religious vocation and Kathleen is a Saturday-night-Sunday-morning thing."

"Hear, hear," Kathleen shouts, I'll drink to that!" She raises her beer glass and out comes what I think is a Rumi poem she's taken some liberties with: "Making love together/getting warmer and warmer/should I throw off this old overcoat of skin/why bother, both worlds are here."

Her recitation sets off a conversation about 21st century spirituality, which Dan, who has a Ph.D. in theology, describes in mock-stentorian tones as: "Coming down from the monastery and the mountain top, we co-create with God to make this world heaven." I ask Dan if he's ever read Elvis's favorite book, ***The Impersonal Life***, which defines spirituality in much the same way as Dan has. He hasn't, so I give a quick summary. Dan is surprised by the content of the book, but even more by Elvis.

"Who knew?" he says.

****

When we return, the moon is so bright we don't even need a flashlight to get to camp. At the bottom of the steps, I stop and look up. There are no outside electric lights here and the sky glitters with stars. Suddenly, streaks of pink, green, and white shimmer across the night. "Northern lights!" Allyn shouts. "I haven't seen them in three years." He leaps up with his arms extended, again and again, as if he's trying to catch them. "So are you cold or are you dancing?" I tease. He smiles. I'm freezing and starting to shiver.

Allyn notices my shaking. "Hey, let's get inside." he says, gently pushing me towards the cabin door. He starts rummaging around in the kitchen and asking if I want hot cocoa or maybe brandy. He's always such a good host, but I want something different. Our conversation from a few days ago emboldens me. I take his hand and lead him to his bunk bed. We lie down face to face; our noses touch. I can feel the air moving through us as if we are breathing each other. Allyn pulls me closer and puts his surprisingly warm hand under my sweater.

The morning sun rises tenderly in the pale pink sky. I get out of Allyn's bunk quietly. It's so narrow, it's a wonder I didn't fall out during the night. I put on his gigantic lumberman's jacket and go outside to say hello to the sun. A band of light stretches across the water. Wherever I move, it moves with me, like my own stairway to heaven. I start singing, "I'm gonna walk, walk dem golden stairs…" I half expect Elvis to join me, but he doesn't. I shout out to him anyway, "Elvis, I am going to write you a public love letter, so everybody knows who you really are!"

I hear laughter. Is Elvis making fun of my grandiosity? I turn. Allyn is standing in the cabin door. The sunlight haloes his silver hair and even his ratty red longjohns look devilishly debonair. He reaches out his hand to mine and pulls me back into the cabin. I do believe he is inviting me to dance.

Acknowledgments

Grateful thanks to all who made this book possible: Richard Ely, Dwight Allen and Betsy Amster (editing), Paul Thoresen (cover photo) and Marcia Schenkel (computer graphics). Thanks to the long suffering Allyn Roberts and Claudia Melrose who gracefully endured my Elvis obsession. And a special thanks to Malynn Utzinger whose love for me and for Elvis brought this book into being.

About the Author

Willow Harth, BA, MA, MS University of Wisconsin, is a former fourth grade teacher and radio talk show host. She has been a partner at Omega Psychology Center in Madison, WI since 1990.

She calls what she does **Inward Bound**: a thrilling, disillusioning, loving and creative adventure into oneself and back into the world.

"I try (not always successfully) to approach the delicate work of relating to another person depth-to-depth with excitement and humility. The excitement comes from being with someone on a quest for wholeness and wellbeing. The humility arises because, although I am steeped in psychotherapeutic tools from cognitive behavioral therapy and the science of emotional intelligence to Buddhist meditation and the tarot, I hesitate to straightjacket anyone in "one size fits all" answers. My intention is to allow healing modalities to arise spontaneously as we explore inner and outer worlds together. The presence I hope permeates the air we breathe is that of the contemporary Jewish mystic, Martin Buber. "Everyone waits shyly and expectantly for the 'YES' from another. For it is from one person to another that the heavenly bread of self-being is passed."

www.ingramcontent.com/pod-product-compliance
Lightning Source LLC
Chambersburg PA
CBHW071516040426
42444CB00008B/1670